Bill Neal's Southern Cooking

Bill Neal's
SOUTHERN COOKING

Revised and Enlarged Edition

The University of North Carolina Press

Chapel Hill | London

Library of Congress Cataloging-in-Publication Data
Neal, Bill.
    [Southern cooking]
    Bill Neal's southern cooking. — Rev. and enl. ed.
        p.   cm.
    Bibliography: p.   Includes index.
    ISBN 0-8078-1859-3 (alk. paper). — ISBN 0-8078-4255-9 (pbk. : alk. paper)
    1. Cookery, American—Southern style.   I. Title.   II. Title:
Southern cooking.
TX715.2.S68N42   1989   641.5975—dc19   88-37258
                                                                        CIP

The paper in this book meets the guidelines for permanence and durability of the Committee on Production Guidelines for Book Longevity of the Council on Library Resources.

93 92 91 90 89   5 4 3 2 1

Excerpt from "No Place for You, My Love" in *The Bride of the Innisfallen and Other Stories,* copyright 1955, 1983 by Eudora Welty. Reprinted by permission of Harcourt Brace Jovanovich, Inc.

Excerpt from "Why I Live at the P.O.," copyright 1941, 1969 by Eudora Welty. Reprinted from her volume *A Curtain of Green and Other Stories* by permission of Harcourt Brace Jovanovich, Inc.

Excerpt from "The Petrified Woman" from *The Collected Stories of Caroline Gordon* copyright 1961, 1963, 1977, 1981 by Caroline Gordon. Reprinted by permission of Farrar, Straus, Giroux, Inc.

Excerpt from *The Member of the Wedding* by Carson McCullers, copyright 1946 by Carson McCullers; copyright renewed 1974 by Floria V. Lasky. Reprinted by permisson of Houghton Mifflin Company.

Excerpt from Carson McCullers, *The Ballad of the Sad Café and Collected Short Stories,* copyright 1936, 1941, 1942, 1943, 1950, 1955, by Carson McCullers. Reprinted by permission of Houghton Mifflin Company.

Excerpt from Thomas Wolfe, *Look Homeward, Angel* copyright 1929 Charles Scribner's Sons; copyright renewed 1957 Edward C. Aswell, as administrator C.T.A. of the Estate of Thomas Wolfe and/or Fred W. Wolfe. Reprinted by permission of Charles Scribner's Sons.

Excerpt from *North Toward Home* copyright 1982 by Willie Morris. Reprinted by permission of Yoknapatawpha Press.

Excerpt from *The Grass Harp* copyright 1951 by Truman Capote. Reprinted by permission of Random House, Inc.

Excerpt from *Foxfire,* Winter 1976, vol. 10, no. 4, p. 294, copyright 1976 The Foxfire Fund, Inc. Reprinted with the permission of Eliot Wigginton for the Foxfire Fund.

For Ellie and Jim Ferguson

Contents

Acknowledgments

My thanks are due to

My mother and grandmothers who nourished the heart as well as the body at the table

My children—Matthew, Elliott, and Madeline—who ate whatever I put in front of them when all they really wanted was hamburgers

Catherine Fogle, who got me out of the classroom and into the kitchen

Maxine Mills and Julia Stockton, who continually offer friendship

Sharon Ryan, who has been always supportive

Don Rodan

Whitney Hyder More

The staff of the Davis Library at the University of North Carolina at Chapel Hill and Ms. Catherine Sadler of the Charleston Library Society, for help in research

Notes on Ingredients and Techniques

1. Baking powder is of the double-acting variety.

2. Butter is unsalted.

3. Eggs are 2 ounces (57 g), called "large" in the store.

4. Flour is of low gluten content. If southern brands such as Martha White or White Lily are not available in your area, mix cake and regular flour half and half for quick breads such as biscuits.

5. Salt is kosher-style flake salt with no additives, except in pickling and preserving. For these processes you *must* use "pickling salt." It, too, has no additives (which would discolor your pickles) but is a very fine grain and will not measure the same as the larger-grained, kosher-style salt.

6. Sidemeat—*see page 94.*

7. Stock for sauces is always best when prepared at home. For long-term storage, freeze it in 1-cup (235 ml) quantities, and thaw what is needed at cooking time. If you do not have the time to prepare stock, try to find a good commercial brand. When using *any* commercial stock be cautious about adding salt, because these preparations usually contain it to excess.

8. Tomatoes (blanched, peeled, and seeded) are prepared as follows: Drop the tomatoes into a large pot of boiling water for about 10 seconds to loosen their skins for peeling. Drain into a colander and cool under cold water. With a sharp paring knife remove the skin and cut the tomatoes in half crosswise. Gently squeeze each half in your hand to remove the seeds and pulp. For a yield of 2 cups (475 ml), you will need three large tomatoes.

9. *See* section on equipment needed for information on all pots, pans, and utensils used in the recipes.

Bill Neal's Southern Cooking

Introduction

So they rested at the table, for the way they ate their meals, this summer, was in rounds: they would eat awhile and then let the food have a chance to spread out and settle inside their stomachs, a little later they would start in again. F. Jasmine crossed her knife and fork on her empty plate, and began to question Berenice about a matter that had bothered her.

"Tell me. Is it just us who call this hopping-john? Or is it known by that name through all the country? It seems a strange name somehow."

"Well, I have heard it called various things," said Berenice.

"What?"

"Well, I have heard it called peas and rice. Or rice and peas and pot-liquor. Or hopping-john. You can vary and take your pick."

"But I'm not talking about this town," F. Jasmine said. "I mean in other places. I mean through all the world. I wonder what the French call it."

Carson McCullers, *The Member of the Wedding*

I wanted to write a cookbook that would reveal something more than just what is consumed by hungry people in the southeastern United States. Nowadays, what may be consumed in the South may have been baked in Omaha. But true southerners hold historical and cultural bonds to heart, above geography; they remain southern wherever they are—New York, Chicago, Paris, London—and their food is part of their cultural identity. In writing this book, I have surveyed the cooking of twelve states: Maryland, the Virginias, the Carolinas, Georgia, Florida, Alabama, Mississippi, Louisiana, Tennessee, and Kentucky. So many different traditions and cooking styles prevail throughout this area that it seems outlandish to consider Louisiana Cajun and refined Maryland plantation cooking in the same context, for the fiery gusto of the former is certainly at odds with the suave elegance of the latter. But in one context, that of southern history, it all fits: this confluence of three cultures—Western European, African, and native American—meeting, clashing, and ultimately melding into one unique identity, one hybrid society, which was changed forever by civil war in the 1860s. The best legacy of that society is what still makes some of us southerners—the architecture, the literature, the food, the continuity of man and nature that shapes our perceptions.

I had to go abroad to appreciate the mystery of food and its rituals in my native southland. The mythic proportions of a bouillabaisse seemed to belong only to other, more exotic cultures, surely not to the prosaic rural and small town life I grew up in. But in France, in the marketplaces and restaurants, and the Arlesian kitchen of M. and Mme Bertaudon, I found patterns and cycles that felt wonderfully comfortable. The fixed patterns of daily meals, the weekly cycles, the seasonal and holiday celebrations told me more about a Frenchman and what he valued than any anthropological treatise could. Each morning in Arles, M. Bertaudon toasted the sun in ancient Provençal with milk and coffee. In early March, great platters of asparagus assured us all the mistral would pass, that days would lengthen. No feast day of the church passed unnoticed: we drank to every saint and never went to mass. In Beaucaire, I met a famous Resistance hero who was still resisting; in the Roman cellar beneath his house he distilled his own *pastis* and poured from the very bottles his father had used. We ate olives planted by seventeenth-century ancestors. A man was sharing his hope for the future, his ties to the past every time he shared a drink, a meal.

I was at home there; the rituals of southern life translated beautifully into the French. My tie to the land had been just as great; the tiny radishes my sister grew in late February were as eagerly anticipated as Argenteuil asparagus. Autumn meant still, warm quail in my father's hunting coat pockets and rabbits lured into my brother's homemade boxes by the scent of vanilla. A caramel cake meant a family birthday, pickled peaches meant Sunday dinner, *after* church. Cooter stew bespoke many mysteries. We children were horrified by the terrapin, a prehistoric hissing monster penned for a week or more in Uncle Skinny's backyard, awaiting execution. There was a secret recipe; only adult males were granted the invitation to sup. At some point I realized my food always had been telling who I was, when, and where; how I felt about my family, and how I related to nature. I saw it first in the lives of people whose language, customs, and culture were foreign, but whose values were mine, before I saw the richness in my, my family's, my region's life.

A larger history exists behind the personal one; in the South the history of the region is all pervasive and embraces the cuisine. Southern food is not just food cooked south of the Mason-Dixon line. It is a product of time and people as well as place. From 1607 to 1860, European, African, and native American cultures accepted and modified each other's agricultural, dietary, and social customs and molded them into a distinct regional cuisine. The cooking, like the society it reflected, was never homogeneous, but it was a synthesis of the major forces behind it. The Civil War changed life in the South drastically. The postwar collapse of the economy halted this melding trend. By the time the cooking began to change again, technology was the major force, not the interplay of culture and custom. The gas stove, refrigerator, modern transportation—all improved the living conditions and changed southern food, but diluted the regional life-styles. The South reentered the nation and changed its own diet.

The recipes in this collection reflect the historical makeup of southern culture. The traditional cuisines of western Europe were practiced in the South by immigrants from England, Scotland, Ireland, Germany, Spain, and especially France. These settlers brought domesticated animals (dairy cattle, swine, and chickens) and their cooking techniques. Africans brought important crops such as field peas, okra, eggplant, peanuts, and yams. Both black and white newcomers relied on the native diet and agriculture: corn, of course, in all its forms, pumpkins, squashes, beans, sassafras filé, a wealth of game and fish, black walnuts, and hickory nuts.

Although southern cooking is born of these three parents—European, African, and native American—not every recipe here combines the culinary aspects of all three cultures. A few dishes belong squarely to one tradition: wine jelly is distinctly English and was prepared in the South with no more than individual variation from the original. Spoon bread, though, is based on the native staple, corn. The soufflé technique is European, and it was black expertise that combined ingredients and technique for this aristocratic favorite. What makes a dish southern is its complete acceptance by the southern community and its general recognition as a southern food. Modern examples make this clear: today, hot dogs are not thought of as German; they are considered thoroughly American, despite their origin. Pizza, meanwhile, is more widely consumed than are frankfurters, yet is still considered Italian, that is, foreign, food. This is the sort of cultural identification test I have given to all the recipes here. Historically, all these recipes existed in some easily recognizable form before 1860. Because most recipe writing of the seventeenth, eighteenth, and nineteenth centuries is sketchy at best, I have not been interested in facsimile recipes. Rather, what you will find in this book are imaginative and original reconstructions of historical dishes that were prepared in the antebellum South.

Two major southern ports, Charleston and New Orleans, contributed so many original dishes and so influenced the entire region that any book on southern food must do them homage, at the risk of slighting lesser-known cooking. Both cities developed splendid markets that married the land and the sea. The cultural mixes were dynamic— English, Spanish, West Indian, especially French and African; and wherever the refinement of the French technique has met the flash of the African palate, the result has invariably been exciting cooking. Almost as important, though less well known, is the cooking of the inland settlers—those from Scotland, Ireland, and Germany. These pioneer culinary traditions receive some long-overdue credit here.

Not long ago I read that to judge from southern cookbooks published in recent times, one would assume beef Stroganoff was a traditional dish. My heart sank. The dishes herein are my rebuttal of that assumption and my affirmation of an active southern heritage. I want to know what season it is, what day it is, where I live, and how I got there; nature has a beautiful and perfect order of which we are all only a small part, and never lords. I want to be a subject to the mystery of this world, and I can do so, in part, by celebrating it at my table, with those I love.

Soups, Gumbo, and Stews

There was the same scene every Saturday at Foché's! A scene to have aroused the guardians of the peace in a locality where such commodities abound. And all on account of the mammoth pot of gumbo that bubbled, bubbled, bubbled out in the open air. Foché in shirt sleeves, fat, red, and enraged, swore and reviled, and stormed at old black Douté for her extravagance. He called her every kind of name of every kind of animal that suggested itself to his lurid imagination. And every fresh invective that he fired at her she hurled it back at him while into the pot went the chickens and the pans-full of minced ham, and the fist-fulls of onion and sage and piment rouge and piment vert. If he wanted her to cook for pigs he had only to say so. She knew how to cook for pigs and she knew how to cook for people of les Avoyelles.

Kate Chopin, "A Night in Acadie"

Soups, like most parts of southern cooking, are regional dishes. I can think of only two that are common to the entire South—the rich broth from a fat hen garnished with the chopped meat and plump rice grains and the farmer's-style vegetable soup chock-full of tomatoes, onions, carrots, peppers, beans, corn, and okra; neither is substantially different from its cousins served throughout the country. But locally, lesser-known soups claim preeminence and reflect more of the forces that created southern cooking. I always look for the native pumpkin in a soup in the piedmont of Virginia and North Carolina. Africans brought the peanut and eggplant, and both are featured in soups where blacks have lived in large numbers. The suave elegance of she-crab soup is practically a symbol for the sophisticated city of Charleston; those wild-looking stuffed heads in a crayfish bisque are a testament to Cajun gusto.

The five examples of grand stews are all public dishes. I have never seen gumbo or Brunswick stew or any of the others prepared for a single family meal. Most frequently, these stews are used to re-create and acknowledge a sense of extended family or community. Many a fire truck has been bought and paid for in rural areas through money raised at a Brunswick stew or burgoo dinner. These country meals are eagerly anticipated; sons and daughters who have left family farms return from the cities and towns to renew old ties.

A large iron pot set over an open fire is the preferred and traditional method for all these stews. One recipe for Brunswick stew begins: "First of all, set the alarm clock for 4:00 A.M. When it goes off in the morning, get up, go outside, build and light the fire, then let it burn down evenly. Put iron pot on fire with 6 gallons of water in it" (*Hand-Me-Down Cookbook*).

Fifteen thousand hungry tourists converge on the two thousand citizens of Grifton, North Carolina, for the Grifton Shad Festival each spring. They come for muddle. The official festival recipe says: "Stew can be cooked inside in an ordinary pot, or outdoors in an iron pot over a gas burner. It's good either way. When cooked outside men are usually the cooks." The men cooks, freed from any debilitating association with the kitchen, are often competitive and even arrogant, asserting the superiority of whatever secret methods they have mastered in preparing any of the stews. They know the success of the stew will be reflected not only in its taste but in the respect accorded the cook by the entire community.

It would be impossible to call any of the recipes below definitive without triggering an avalanche of response. The Grifton Shad Festival advises: "Ingredients are seldom measured and seasonings are added according to taste. More or less of each ingredient can be used." Whatever the name—from gumbo to burgoo—these are intensely local dishes delineating and reflecting traditional communities. The effort required of the cooks is justified as an expression, affirmation, and extension of their values. But finally it is undoubtedly exhausting. The cook who started his fire at 4:00 A.M. may be too tired to taste his own wares. That recipe ends, "Cook stew until 1:30 P.M. Call 'Maw' to dip up stew. Go into quiet house, leaving all the folks around the pot eating stew, and take a nice, long relaxed nap" (*Hand-Me-Down Cookbook*).

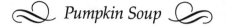 *Pumpkin Soup*

Around the stalks of maize in the pre-European gardens of the native Americans wove the vines and tendrils of the cucurbits, better known to us as the squashes, gourds, and pumpkins. Their extensive growth and broad leaves provided a sheltering for moisture from the sun's rays and hindered weed seed germination. The colonists adopted the squashes for their kitchens, especially the pumpkin. They boiled it as a vegetable, puréed and baked it as a savory custard, sweetened it for pies, and preserved it as a jam or chutneylike conserve. In Louisiana, pumpkin was baked in its rind and eaten with butter or gravy. A delicious soup was made from it also, which is not as common in the United States as formerly. Other traditional cuisines of this hemisphere such as the Mexican have retained it, and the French and Spanish have adopted it with enthusiasm.

Yields 2 quarts

1½ pounds (675 g) peeled fresh pumpkin, cubed, or 1 pound (450 g) canned, unflavored pumpkin
3 tablespoons (45 g) butter
½ cup (118 ml) chopped scallions, white part only
½ cup (118 ml) chopped celery
½ cup (118 ml) chopped carrots
1 garlic clove, chopped
3 cups (705 ml) chicken stock

1 cup (235 ml) canned Italian tomatoes, chopped, with juice
¼ teaspoon dried red pepper flakes
¼ teaspoon white pepper
⅛ teaspoon freshly grated nutmeg
2 cups (475 ml) half-and-half
Green tops of scallions, sliced very thin

Note on fresh pumpkin: Discard seeds and strings of interior, cut into cubes and peel. Sprinkle with water, place in a baking dish, cover tightly, and bake at 325°F (163°C) for 45 minutes or until very tender.

Recommended equipment: A 3-quart (3 L) saucepan; food mill, blender, or food processor.

Melt the butter in the saucepan and sauté gently the scallions, celery, and carrots. Add the garlic, stir briefly, and add the stock, tomatoes, and pumpkin. Season with red pepper flakes, white pepper, and nutmeg. Cook slowly for 1 hour. Remove from heat, let cool slightly, and purée until texture is very smooth.

To serve: reheat gently with the half-and-half. Garnish with the thinly sliced green tops of the scallions.

❧ Eggplant Soup ❧

Eggplant came to the American South from Africa, Africa in turn having received it from the Orient through the Portuguese trade. Its place in traditional southern cooking reflects its journey. In the piedmont and mountain regions of the South, settled by farmers mainly of Scotch, Irish, and German backgrounds, who were not major slaveholders, eggplant was rarely seen. In and around Charleston and New Orleans—cities with large black populations—eggplant became established in the local cuisine. Charlestonians still call it Guinea squash, after its source.

This soup is excellent cold, as a summer aspic. If it does not set up on its own, add unflavored gelatin—1 package dissolved and stirred into the warm stock should suffice. (Remember to remove as much fat as possible from the surface of the soup before chilling.) Garnish with finely shredded crisp lettuce and lemon wedges.

Yields 2 quarts

¼ cup (60 ml) bacon fat
¾ cup (180 ml) finely chopped onion
½ cup (118 ml) finely chopped celery
½ cup (118 ml) finely chopped green bell pepper
1 cup (235 ml) finely chopped tomatoes (blanched, peeled, and seeded; see page xiv)

2 cups (475 ml) diced eggplant
2 garlic cloves, minced
½ teaspoon curry powder
¼ teaspoon dried thyme
¼ teaspoon dried basil
Salt
Freshly ground black pepper
4 cups (950 ml) chicken stock
Fresh parsley, chopped

Recommended equipment: A 4-quart (4 L) covered saucepan.

Heat the bacon fat in the saucepan and add the onion, celery, and green pepper. Sauté over high heat, stirring, for 6 minutes. Reduce heat to medium high and add tomato and eggplant. Stir well for 3 minutes, add garlic, curry powder, thyme, basil, salt and pepper, and cover.

Reduce heat to medium and let vegetables sweat (shaking the pan vigorously from time to time to prevent sticking or burning) for 5 to 7 minutes. When the vegetables are tender add chicken stock and simmer for 30 minutes. Garnish with freshly chopped parsley.

∾ Peanut Soup ∽

The cuisines of warm lands around the globe from Africa to Asia have incorporated the South American native, the peanut. The southeastern United States is no exception. Peanut soup is a hallmark of eastern Virginia cooking and part of the legacy of African cooks who introduced the legume (after receiving it from the Portuguese slave traders) to North America.

Yields 1½ quarts

2 tablespoons (30 g) butter
1 cup (235 ml) chopped onion
½ cup (118 ml) chopped celery
1 cup (235 ml) roasted, shelled,
   unsalted peanuts
2 garlic cloves, minced
2 tablespoons flour

¼ teaspoon red pepper flakes
   (or more)
½ teaspoon dried thyme
4 cups (950 ml) chicken stock
½ cup (118 ml) heavy cream
Salt and freshly ground black
   pepper

Garnish

1 cup (235 ml) thinly sliced okra
2 tablespoons cornmeal
½ teaspoon salt

¼ teaspoon freshly ground black
   pepper
3 tablespoons vegetable oil
½ cup (118 ml) sliced scallions

Recommended equipment: A 3-quart (3 L) saucepan; food mill, blender, or food mill attachment for electric mixer; fine-mesh strainer; 10-inch (25 cm) cast-iron skillet or enameled cast-iron sauté pan.

Melt the butter over medium high heat in the saucepan and sauté the onion and celery until soft. Add the peanuts and the minced garlic, stirring well. Add flour and cook until it browns lightly, stirring constantly. Season with red pepper flakes and thyme, slowly pour in the stock, stirring well, and simmer for 25 minutes until the peanuts are tender. Allow to cool and purée the soup using a food mill, blender, or attachment for an electric mixer. Pass the purée through a fine-mesh strainer. Stir in the heavy cream and season with salt and freshly ground black pepper. Reheat gently to serve.

For the garnish, rinse the sliced okra under running cold water and drain. Combine the cornmeal, salt, and pepper, and toss with the okra to coat it lightly. Heat the oil in the skillet or sauté pan over high heat until almost smoking. Reduce heat slightly and add the okra, flash-frying and shaking the pan, until the okra browns lightly. Add the scallions all at once and cook until just wilted. Remove from pan with a slotted spoon and top each bowl of soup with some of the vegetables.

 Crab Soup

The blue crabs of the southeastern coastal waters are known by scientists as *Callinectes sapidus* and, more aesthetically, by certain native Indians and students of Greek as "beautiful swimmers." Those meeting these crustaceans under less auspicious circumstances are more likely to recall the etymological associations of crab with "scratch" and "claw," and Nevyll's vivid image: "those crabsnowted bestes, those ragyng feends of hell." Beyond words, blue crabs find immortality in the dishes of the coastal cities. Charlestonians insist on the female crab for their celebrated she-crab soups, the eggs adding richness and finesse. A mock egg garnish of sieved hard-boiled egg yolk is added when there is a paucity of females, as suggested below.

The Charleston-style soup is a masterpiece of delicacy—as initial flavors fade on the palate, others bloom, heightened by the slowly growing awareness of cayenne and an aromatic vegetable base. No two tastes of the soup register the same, the palate is never bored. This, one of the most elegant of all southern soups, can be used as a smaller part of a formal menu, or as the focus of a lunch or informal supper.

Yields 2 quarts

6 tablespoons (90 g) butter	1 cup (235 ml) finely chopped
½ cup (118 ml) finely chopped	scallions, white part only
celery	(reserve green ends for
2½ cups (590 ml) milk	garnish, if desired)
2½ cups (590 ml) chicken stock	6 tablespoons flour

Salt if needed

1/4 teaspoon freshly grated nutmeg

1/4 teaspoon white pepper

1/8 to 1/4 teaspoon (or more) ground cayenne

1 cup (235 ml) heavy cream

1 pound (450 g) picked crabmeat, backfin or special, not claw

2 to 4 tablespoons (30 to 60 ml) Amontillado sherry

Optional: yolks of 2 hard-boiled eggs; scallion tops, very thinly sliced; fresh parsley, chopped.

Recommended equipment: A 3-quart (3 L) or larger heavy saucepan with a cover, 1½-quart (1½ L) saucepan, wire whisk.

In the large saucepan, melt the butter over medium heat and add the celery. Reduce heat to low, cover pan, and gently sweat the celery for ten minutes, taking care not to brown it. While the celery is cooking, heat the milk and chicken stock together in the smaller saucepan over medium heat, bringing the liquid to just below a simmer. When the celery has finished cooking, add the scallions and stir for one minute. Sprinkle the flour evenly over the vegetables and continue to stir gently. Again, do not allow the mixture to brown, but provide enough heat for the roux to bubble gently for 3 minutes. Slowly add the warmed milk and stock, stirring with a whisk. Taste for salt: if you are using canned stock, there probably will be no need for any more. Add the white pepper, cayenne, and nutmeg. Simmer for 20 minutes.

Just before serving, add the heavy cream and bring to the boil. Using a wooden spoon, stir in the crabmeat gently. Season with sherry and serve immediately.

To make an optional garnish, mimicking she-crab eggs, pass hard-boiled yolks through a fine-mesh strainer. Sprinkle over the top of the soup with very thinly sliced raw scallion tops or freshly chopped parsley, or both.

Crayfish Bisque

Crayfish, crawfish, crawdad, crawdaddy are what the French call écrevisse, and what the Cajuns tout as a cultural symbol. I shall never forget my first foray into Cajun country. Hand-lettered placards in country store windows announcing "Hot Boudin" or "Fais-do-do Saturday" were a sure sign we had crossed a boundary greater than the

Mississippi. In New Iberia, we raced past the Lady Evangeline Funeral Home on our way to Breaux Bridge, the reputed crayfish capital of the country. The restaurant our Mississippi friends had recommended was closed; we were on our own. One-half mile out of town, next to a sluggish brown bayou, I knew we had found the right spot. A ramshackle white frame building was settling under its burden: a twenty-foot-long red fiberglass crayfish. The sign read only "French music." In the window, no Mobil stars, no praise from Mimi Sheraton, just an autographed picture of Tammy Wynette. Inside, we sat down to an orgy of crayfish—boiled, fried, sautéed, baked. But to start the feast, the waitress acclaimed the bisque; to get it, we had to decipher the insistent, repeated query. Finally, the light dawned; she was asking, in Cajun French, "Combien de têtes?"—how many stuffed heads did we want in our soup?

Yields 6 servings

3 dozen live crayfish

The stock

6 cups (1410 ml) water
1 cup (235 ml) chopped onion
1/2 cup (118 ml) chopped celery
1/2 cup (118 ml) chopped carrot
1 garlic clove
1 bay leaf

1/2 teaspoon dried thyme
1/8 teaspoon ground cloves
3 large sprigs fresh parsley
1 dried red pepper pod
1 teaspoon salt

The roux

3 tablespoons (45 g) butter
3 tablespoons flour

Aromatic vegetables and seasonings

1 cup (235 ml) thinly sliced
  scallions
1/2 cup (118 ml) fresh, finely
  chopped tomatoes (blanched,
  peeled, and seeded; see page
  xiv)

1/4 cup (60 ml) finely chopped
  green bell pepper
1/4 teaspoon white pepper
1/4 teaspoon ground cayenne
1/2 teaspoon sugar
1 teaspoon paprika

Soups

Stuffing for heads

3 tablespoons (45 g) butter
1/4 cup (60 ml) minced onion
1/4 cup (60 ml) minced celery
1/4 cup (60 ml) minced green bell
  pepper
1 tablespoon chopped fresh
  parsley

2/3 cup (160 ml) stale white bread
  crumbs
1 egg
2 tablespoons water (optional)
Salt and freshly ground black
  pepper

Sautéing of heads

4 tablespoons (60 g) butter
1/2 cup (118 ml) flour
1/2 teaspoon salt
1/8 teaspoon white pepper
1/4 teaspoon paprika
Cold water

Recommended equipment: An 8-quart (8 L) stockpot, slotted spoon, 1½-quart (1½ L) heavy-bottomed or enameled saucepan, wire whisk, 12-inch (30 cm) cast-iron skillet or enameled cast-iron sauté pan.

Wash the crayfish well under running cold water.

Combine all the ingredients for the stock and bring to a boil over high heat. Reduce heat and simmer for 20 minutes. Add the live crayfish and cook about 5 minutes, or until just done. Remove the crayfish with tongs or slotted spoon and let cool while stock continues to simmer.

Separate heads and tails of crayfish, reserving 18 heads. Peel tails and reserve meat, adding shells back to the simmering stock. Wash the reserved heads well, drain, and hold aside for stuffing. Strain stock after it has simmered with the shells for 20 minutes; discard debris.

For the roux, melt the butter in the saucepan and whisk in the flour. Cook slowly over medium heat, watching it carefully and stirring often, until it turns a deep, dark brown, roughly the color of dark brown sugar. This should take about 25 to 30 minutes—the color must change *very* slowly or the result will be a bitter-tasting roux. Remove from heat. Immediately add the scallions, tomato, pepper, white pepper, cayenne, sugar, and paprika. Stir well and slowly add the strained stock, return to heat, and simmer for 30 minutes. Add peeled crayfish tails just before serving.

Meanwhile, prepare the stuffing for the heads. In a skillet or sauté pan, melt the 3 tablespoons of butter over low heat. Lightly sauté the onion, celery, and pepper until tender. Remove from heat, let cool briefly, and turn into a bowl. Stir in the parsley and bread crumbs. Beat the egg well and add it to the stuffing with additional water, if needed. Season with salt and lots of freshly ground black pepper. Stuff the reserved heads with this mixture.

Wipe the skillet or sauté pan clean with a paper towel, and melt the 4 tablespoons of butter in it. Combine the flour, salt, white pepper, and paprika in a bowl. Dip the stuffed heads in cold water and then in the flour. Sauté gently on all sides over medium heat until golden brown.

To serve: Place the hot, sautéed heads in warmed soup plates. Pour the soup in the dishes and serve immediately.

 Oyster Stew

Before the days of freon, so many foods signaled such a particular time of year that they were symbols of the seasons more reliable than any calendar. Even today asparagus heralds spring more surely than any number of robins; blackberries mean July, hot weather, and chiggers. Persimmons avenge themselves on those who try to jump into fall. And when the months of cooler weather—the "R" months—return, so does the oyster.

Before acceptance of refrigerated food transport (for meat only, first, and that was in the 1880s), inland food supplies depended on the weather. Even after the first frost warm spells threatened the integrity of almost any product, especially seafood. Only December, though the fourth "R" month, guaranteed enough sustained cold weather for shipping. Then, from Baltimore, to Charleston, to New Orleans, oysters were shoveled onto the flat backs of horse-drawn wagons and packed down in wet straw and seaweed for an inland journey some-times lasting two weeks or more. Far from the coast, oysters became a symbol of the arrival of the winter holiday season, appearing in the markets by Christmas Eve and on the tables that night as oyster stew.

A basic southern oyster stew highlights the simplest ingredients: 3 parts milk, 1 part heavy cream, heated, with 2 parts shucked oysters added and poached lightly, seasoned only with fresh black pepper and whole butter—salted crackers the only accompaniment. A more elabo-rate version follows, which celebrates a winter harvest of watercress (many southerners guard the secret location of their personal wild cress springs as if they were gold mines).

Yields 4 to 6 servings

3 tablespoons (45 g) butter
²⁄₃ cup (160 ml) finely chopped onion
½ cup (118 ml) finely chopped celery
¼ cup (60 ml) raw long grain rice
2½ cups (590 ml) chicken stock
1 pint (475 ml) whole shucked oysters, drained

2½ cups (590 ml) milk or cream
1 tablespoon (15 g) butter
1 cup (235 ml) chopped watercress
½ cup (118 ml) thinly sliced scallions
1 teaspoon salt
Freshly ground black pepper
Watercress for garnish

Recommended equipment: A 3-quart (3 L) or larger saucepan; food mill, food processor, blender, or food mill attachment for mixer; fine-mesh strainer; 1½ quart (1½ L) saucepan with lid.

Beforehand: Melt the 3 tablespoons of butter in the saucepan and sauté the onion and celery until lightly colored. When tender, add raw rice and stir well for 3 minutes. Add chicken stock and cook gently over low heat for 35 minutes, stirring occasionally. Purée this mixture in a food mill, blender, or food processor, and pass through a strainer so you are sure that the mixture is perfectly smooth. Set aside until shortly before you are ready to finish the stew.

When ready to serve, add milk or cream to puréed rice mixture and bring to a simmer in the saucepan. Melt the 1 tablespoon of butter over low heat in the small saucepan and add the watercress and scallions. Toss several times and cover tightly to steam until just wilted and still bright green. Add the drained oysters to the soup and poach them for 4 to 5 minutes until the edges curl. *Do not boil.* Add seasonings, quickly stir in the watercress and scallions, and serve immediately. Garnish with watercress.

∾ Shrimp and Crab Gumbo ∾

Gumbo means seafood to most people, but in Mississippi, Alabama, and Louisiana as many gumbos bubble away as there are pots. Chicken, turkey, duck, ham, sausage, and even venison end up in the soup with the holy trinity of Cajun cooking: onions, peppers, and celery. There is also a little-known specialty made of leafy green vege-tables—gumbo aux herbes. The mystery of a great gumbo is contained in its smoky roux, slowly and reverentially browned to just this side of scorching. Another thickener binds the soup with a slickness peculiar to southern cooking—an okra thickener from the African cooks, as below, or a final dash of sassafras filé from the original native cuisine.

Yields 10 servings

Gumbo thickener

7 medium, ripe tomatoes (blanched, peeled, and seeded; see page xiv), chopped to yield 4 cups (950 ml)

4 cups (950 ml) very thinly sliced okra
3 tablespoons (45 g) lard or bacon fat

Roux

3½ tablespoons (53 g) lard
6 tablespoons flour

Seafood

6 live hard-shelled blue crabs
2½ pounds (1125 g) shrimp in the shell

Stock

2½ quarts (2½ L) water
2 bay leaves
1 dried red pepper pod
1½ teaspoons dried thyme
2 teaspoons salt

½ teaspoon freshly ground black pepper
½ teaspoon Tabasco
Shrimp and crab shells

Aromatic vegetables

3 tablespoons peanut oil
2 medium onions, chopped (to yield 2 cups or 475 ml)
1½ green bell peppers, chopped (to yield 1½ cups or 355 ml)

3 celery ribs, chopped (to yield 1 cup or 235 ml)
3 garlic cloves, peeled and chopped
1 whole green cayenne pepper, chopped with seeds

Rice

4½ cups (1 L) water
2½ cups (590 ml) raw long grain
   rice
1½ teaspoons salt
4 tablespoons (60 g) butter

Recommended equipment: Two cast-iron skillets or enameled cast-iron sauté pans, one 12 inch (30 cm) and one 8 inch (20 cm); wire whisk; cleaver or very heavy butcher's knife; 8-quart (8 L) (or larger) stockpot; colander; 1½-quart (1½ L) saucepan with lid.

The gumbo thickener

Coarsely chop the tomatoes and set aside.

Remove stems and tips from okra and slice thinly.

Melt the bacon fat or lard in the large skillet or sauté pan over medium heat. Add the okra and stir well for 3 to 4 minutes. Do not allow the okra to brown. Add the chopped tomatoes and continue cooking, uncovered, for about 1 hour over low heat. Stir frequently to prevent sticking.

The roux

While the thickener is cooking, melt the lard over low heat in the smaller skillet or sauté pan and stir in the flour with a whisk. Depending upon your burner, you may increase the heat to medium. However, keep a careful eye on the flour so that it changes color almost imperceptibly. If it starts to color quickly, remove from burner and reduce heat. Burned flour will make a *bitter-tasting* roux. Stir frequently enough to prevent sticking. During this time peel the shrimp and reserve the shells for the stock ingredients, watching the roux at all times. The desired color will be similar to dark brown sugar, and it will take about 25 to 30 minutes to reach this stage. When done, scrape roux into a small bowl with a wooden spoon or spatula and reserve.

Crabmeat

Rinse the live crabs well under cold water. Always handle them from behind—you can do this safely without ever being pinched.

1. Put the crab on its back on a cutting board.

2. Remove the apron—it will separate easily with a quick tug.

3. Flip the crab over and pop off the outer shell, pulling from front to back.

4. Split the crab down the middle with a heavy butcher knife or cleaver.

5. Remove gills on either side and eyes, and rinse under running cold water.

6. Wash out intestinal tract, leaving the pinkish-orange eggs intact.

7. Crack the claws between each joint with the back side of a strong knife.

Reserve the halved crabs in the coldest part of the refrigerator and add the shells to the stock ingredients.

Stock

Combine water, bay, pepper pod, thyme, salt, black pepper, Tabasco, and crab and shrimp shells in the stockpot. Bring to a boil over high heat, reduce heat and simmer for 20 minutes. Strain into a large bowl and discard solids. Reserve.

Aromatic vegetables

Heat the peanut oil in the larger skillet or sauté pan and add the chopped vegetables. Cover and cook over medium-low heat for 20 minutes, taking care not to brown the vegetables. Remove cover and cook off excess liquid for 5 minutes.

Assembly and serving

Add the vegetables to the stockpot. Over medium heat stir in the roux with a whisk until well blended. Slowly add the stock, whisking continuously. Add the gumbo thickener and bring to a boil over high heat, stirring frequently. Reduce heat to a simmer and cook at least 1 hour, and preferably 2.

Near the end of the simmering period, prepare rice by bringing water to a boil, then add rice and salt. Cover and cook over low heat about 25 minutes. Remove from heat, add butter, and keep covered.

Just before serving, bring gumbo stock to a boil. Add the halved crabs and stir well. When liquid returns to a full boil, stir in the shrimp, cover tightly, and immediately turn off the heat. Let sit for 3 to 6 minutes, depending upon the size of the shrimp.

For each serving, put ³⁄₄ cup cooked, buttered rice in a large, heated soup bowl and ladle the steaming hot gumbo over it.

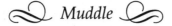 Muddle

A muddle is a very thick fish stew celebrated in eastern Virginia and North Carolina, particularly on the long isolated barrier islands known as the Outer Banks. The customs and foods of the earliest English colonists have been maintained on these Atlantic outposts; linguists study the dialect for its Elizabethan overtones, and anthropologists record the raucous Twelfth Night celebrations. Muddle is the traditional feast of the region whose poor soil yields a meager harvest. The simple vegetables—potatoes, onions, tomatoes—in perfect proportion with the freshest fish achieve the satisfaction sought in all good peasant cooking.

Yields 12 servings

1½ teaspoons dried thyme
2 bay leaves
2 whole cloves
1½ teaspoons (or more) red pepper flakes
½ pound (225 g) sliced bacon cut into 1-inch (2½ cm) squares
3 pounds (1350 g) onions, thinly sliced
3 pounds (1350 g) boiling potatoes, peeled, thinly sliced
½ cup (118 ml) chopped, fresh parsley

3 pounds (1350 g) large, firm white-fleshed nonoily fish fillets cut into cubes 1½ inches (3¾ cm) on each side
Salt
Freshly ground black pepper
1 pound (450 g) canned whole tomatoes, chopped with liquid
Water
2 tablespoons apple cider vinegar
1 dozen very fresh eggs at room temperature

Recommended equipment: A blender or mortar and pestle, Dutch oven.

Preheat oven to 325°F (163°C).
   Pulverize the thyme, bay, cloves, and red pepper flakes to a fine, regular powder, either in a blender or by hand in the mortar, and reserve. Render the bacon gently in the bottom of the casserole until lightly browned. Remove one-half of the bacon and reserve. Divide the onions, potatoes, parsley, fish, pulverized seasonings, and tomatoes with their liquid in two equal portions. Assemble by layering the ingredients in the following order, lightly sprinkling each layer with salt and freshly ground black pepper: onions, potatoes, parsley, fish, seasonings, tomatoes, bacon, onions, potatoes, parsley, fish, season-

ings, and tomatoes. Add just enough cold water to cover, but not swamp, the ingredients. Finally, add the cider vinegar. Bring to a gentle boil on top of the stove over medium heat. Cover tightly and place in the preheated oven. Bake for 1 hour or until the ingredients are just tender.

When the top layer of potatoes is done, the whole will be ready. Return to the top of the stove over medium heat. Break the eggs over the surface as it bubbles. Cover and cook for 4 minutes. The eggs should be lightly poached, the whites set and the yolks still liquid. Serve in warmed bowls with one egg per serving. Accompany with Hushpuppies and Coleslaw (see recipes).

⟨Q⟩ Brunswick Stew ⟨Q⟩

Most folks will agree that Brunswick stew took its name from Brunswick County, Virginia, but that's about all they'll agree on concerning this southern favorite. Despite the apocryphal tales of its invention on a certain date by a certain cook on a wilderness hunt, this stew is clearly in the tradition of the native cooking. All the oldest and most traditional sources agree that game—usually squirrel—simmered over an open fire with corn is the essence of Brunswick stew, reminiscent of various early descriptions of the native dishes, mostly meats and fish boiled with some form of maize. In the autumn, from Maryland to Georgia, the devotees of this hearty meal still stir it slowly and continuously with long oak paddles as it bubbles away in iron pots over hardwood flames.

Yields 8 to 10 servings

1 chicken weighing about 4 pounds (1800 g), poached (see below)
1 rabbit weighing about 2 pounds (900 g), quartered
All giblets: heart, gizzard, and liver from chicken and liver and kidney from rabbit
4 ounces (115 g) pork sidemeat, finely chopped
1½ cups (355 ml) chopped onion

1 cup (235 ml) chopped celery
1 cup (235 ml) carrots, peeled, quartered, and cut into ¾ inch (2 cm) lengths
2 cups (475 ml) finely sliced cabbage
2 garlic cloves, chopped
¾ teaspoon thyme
1 bay leaf
¼ to ½ teaspoon dried red pepper flakes

1³/₄ pounds (800 g) canned
    tomatoes, chopped, with juice
1¹/₄ cups (295 ml) shelled lima
    beans (use very small
    immature beans)
2 cups (475 ml) baking potatoes,
    peeled and cut into ¹/₂ × ¹/₂
    × ³/₄ inch (1 × 1 × 2 cm)
    pieces

2 cups (475 ml) double-cut corn
    (2 large ears)
7 cups (1650 ml) stock and all the
    fat from the chicken
Salt and freshly ground black
    pepper
Additional vegetables in season:
    fresh peas, okra

Note on fresh corn: shuck and silk the corn, removing any damaged portions. Wash in cold water and drain. With a sharp knife cut down the center of each row of kernels, holding the knife blade parallel to the cob. Turn the blade horizontally and shave the kernels into a bowl.

Recommended equipment: Two stockpots, one 8 quart (8 L) and one 16 quart (15 L) are preferable to save time, although one is sufficient.

Poach the chicken according to the master recipe (see page 114). After cooking the chicken for 35 minutes, add the quartered rabbit, all the giblets, and additional water to cover. When done, drain and reserve the stock. When they are cool enough to handle, bone the chicken and rabbit, and chop the meat into 1-inch (2¹/₂ cm) squares. Dice the giblets, and reserve all the meats in a bowl, covered. Reduce the stock to 7 cups, skimming and discarding impurities, but saving the fat.

Render the finely chopped sidemeat in the bottom of a large stock-pot over medium heat. Add the onion, celery, carrot, and cabbage and cook until tender. Add garlic, thyme, bay, and red pepper flakes. Stir in the tomatoes with their juice and bring to a boil, then simmer for 20 minutes. Add the lima beans, potatoes, and corn. Return to the boil and stir in the chopped meats and giblets with the stock and fat. Bring to the boil again, and then simmer until the stew thickens, stirring frequently to prevent scorching. This will take about 1 hour.

Season to taste with salt and freshly ground black pepper. If you have excellent young vegetables such as spring peas or summer okra, these may be added during the last 5 minutes of cooking. Hushpup-pies (see page 27) are an excellent accompaniment to this stew.

❧ Burgoo ❧

Like minestrone and garbure, burgoo is in the tradition of great country stews found all over the world. It is completely southern in its broad use of regional vegetables—okra, fresh corn, tiny limas—but unique in its call for mutton. Neither mutton nor lamb has been consumed widely in the South in the past century, though the diaries and kitchen books of early settlers often mention them. Today, a few towns in Virginia still feature "sheep stew" at fund-raising suppers, but it is western Kentucky that claims mutton as its culinary badge. In Owensboro, Kentucky, there is an annual festival for tens of thousands who come for barbecued mutton and burgoo. And, a little to the west, in Arkansas, it's said—though Kentuckians disagree—they make a pretty good burgoo as well.

Yields 16 servings

1 pound (450 g) pork shoulder
1 pound (450 g) veal shank
1 pound (450 g) beef shank or ox tail
2 pounds (900 g) mutton or lamb breast
6 quarts (5¼ L) water
1 teaspoon dried sage
2 teaspoons dried thyme
2 whole bay leaves
2 dried red pepper pods
4 teaspoons salt
¾ teaspoon freshly ground black pepper
1 hen weighing about 4 pounds (1800 g), with giblets

1 pound (450 g) boiling potatoes, peeled and sliced
1 pound (450 g) onions, peeled and chopped
½ pound (225 g) carrots, peeled and chopped
2 cups (475 ml) chopped cabbage
2 cups (475 ml) tomatoes (blanched, peeled, and seeded; see page xiv), chopped
1 cup (235 ml) lima beans
1½ cups (355 ml) fresh, cut corn
1 cup (235 ml) thinly sliced okra
1½ tablespoons Worcestershire sauce
½ cup (118 ml) fresh, chopped parsley

Recommended equipment: A 16-quart (15 L) stockpot, food grinder if desired.

Combine the pork, veal, beef, and mutton or lamb breast in the large stockpot with the water, sage, thyme, bay, red pepper, salt, and black pepper. Bring to a boil over high heat, reduce heat, and simmer gently for 30 minutes. Add the hen with its giblets—heart, gizzard, and liver. Continue simmering gently for another 1½ hours, or until all the meats are tender. Remove the meats and let them cool.

Bone and chop all the meat, or put it through the coarse blade of a food grinder. Do not use a food processor. Return the meat to the broth and add the potatoes, onions, carrots, cabbage, and tomatoes. Simmer for 30 minutes and add the lima beans. Cook at the barest simmer for 1½ hours. Add the corn, okra, and Worcestershire sauce and cook for an additional 30 minutes. Stir in the fresh parsley, taste for salt and pepper, and serve to a hungry crowd.

Cornmeal, Hominy Grits, Biscuits, and Bread

On winter afternoons, as soon as I came in from school, Catherine hustled open a jar of preserves, while Dolly put a foot high pot of coffee on the stove and pushed a pan of biscuits into the oven.

Truman Capote, *The Grass Harp*

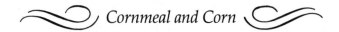 *Cornmeal and Corn*

Every southerner knows the one item distinguishing his diet is corn—fresh, dried, or distilled. He may find hot biscuits in the Midwest, or moist, smoky hams in New England, but he won't find his hushpuppies, spoon bread, or grits. The South is steadfast in its loyalty to the native grain; almost every other cuisine has adopted wheat as the preferred bread-making staple as soon as it became available. Southern cooks, however, held corn and its many breads in the highest regard. Not until the twentieth century did corn breads have a close rival in the general diet.

The native North Americans would have found it heresy to question the supremacy of their staple crop. Etymologically, the word "maize" connoted the idea of the universal mother who sustained life. (Corn, more prosaically, is an Anglo-Saxon word which, in the rest of the English-speaking world, means any hard grain or seed.) Maize did support life in every aspect in pre-European America—as the staple food, as medicine made from the tassels, as shelters made from stalks. In cooking, corn had two forms: the first was raw or cooked green corn; the second was dried corn processed in one of two ways—either ground or soaked in an alkali solution. Ground corn is essentially cornmeal; the coarsest cracked corn was parched and eaten plain, especially on long hunting trips. My father carried this to school wrapped in a piece of paper as a recess-time snack in the 1930s. With some elaboration cornmeal became breads, fritters, and dumplings. Hominy comes from soaking and dehulling the dried corn. The Cherokees cooked hominy whole with pumpkin, beans, and walnuts. A hominy drink, Gv-No-He-Nv, was their symbol of hospitality. (A recipe for whole hominy can be found in the vegetable chapter.) Dried and ground, hominy becomes grits.

The value of corn in North America has not diminished during the five thousand or so years of its cultivation. Exactly where and when corn appeared is not known, but man prized it enough to ensure its continuity. The farmer is essential to the reproduction of corn, a crop dependent on agriculture. No wild corn has ever been found; no known corn can reseed itself. The early English settlers who frittered away their time in a futile search for gold would have done better to pursue the main achievement of Indian agriculture. Now in the United States, corn is the most important food crop; the value of the annual harvest surpasses by far the product of all metal mines or coalfields of the country.

Dog bread is just about the simplest way to consume cornmeal, short of simply parching it and eating it out of the hand. Served hot, with lots of butter, these crisp griddle cakes have a charm that can pair them well with sophisticated beef and pork roasts. Hushpuppies can be as simple as a thick dog bread batter, deep-fried. Usually though, hushpuppies are enriched by milk, eggs, and onions. Baked, a hushpuppy-style batter becomes corn bread, though minus the onion. In its apotheosis, cornmeal takes the form of an elegant soufflé, the fabled spoon bread, a mainstay of the aristocratic southern table.

Either yellow or white cornmeal may be used in the following recipes. Freshness is more important than color or the method of grinding.

Dog Bread

Dog bread is especially good with the pan juices of simple roasts or with greens and plenty of potlikker.

Yields about 16 cakes

1 cup (235 ml) cornmeal
¼ teaspoon salt
1 cup (235 ml) cold water
Bacon fat

Recommended equipment: A 12-inch (30 cm) cast-iron skillet or enameled cast-iron sauté pan.

Combine the cornmeal and salt, and slowly stir in the cold water. Let stand for 5 minutes.

Heat the skillet or sauté pan over medium heat and add enough bacon fat to create a layer ⅛ inch (⅓ cm) deep. Drop the batter by spoonfuls into the hot grease, allowing plenty of room to spread. Turn the cakes when golden and crisp and brown on the opposite side. Serve hot with lots of butter.

Indian Dumplings

These gnocchi-like cornmeal dumplings are commonly cooked in a pot of greens, but may be added to hearty stews or vegetable soups.

Yields 16 dumplings

1 cup (235 ml) cornmeal
1 teaspoon salt
½ cup (118 ml) boiling water or
   boiling stock from the greens
1 teaspoon bacon fat (optional)

Recommended equipment: A small mixing bowl, wooden spoon, slotted spoon.

Combine the dry ingredients in the mixing bowl. Add the boiling liquid very slowly, working the meal well with the back of a wooden spoon. Work in the bacon fat if desired. The dough must be very thick, but wet enough to hold together without cracking. Divide into 16 portions and shape into balls. Flatten into circles approximately 1 inch (2½ cm) across, and ⅜ inch (1 cm) thick. Edges should be smooth, appearing as miniature biscuits. Place on top of the bubbling broth. Cover and cook for about 10 minutes. Serve with greens or along with the soup or stew.

∽ Hushpuppies ∾

These cornmeal fritters are the classic accompaniment for many meals. At outdoor fish fries and pork barbecues (known in the South as pig-pickin's) a pot of bubbling oil hangs over an open flame to ensure the hottest, crispest hushpuppies at just the right moment.

Yields about 4 dozen

1½ cups (355 ml) yellow
　cornmeal
½ cup (61 g) flour
1 teaspoon salt
½ teaspoon sugar
2 tablespoons baking powder
1 teaspoon baking soda
1/16 teaspoon to ⅛ teaspoon
　cayenne pepper

¼ teaspoon freshly ground black
　pepper
2 eggs, beaten and combined
　with sufficient buttermilk to
　make 1¼ cups (295 ml)
2 tablespoons rendered bacon fat
　or melted lard
½ cup (118 ml) finely chopped
　green onion
Peanut oil for frying

Recommended equipment: A 12-inch (30 cm) cast-iron skillet or deep fryer, frying thermometer, slotted spoon, brown paper bag.

Sift all the dry ingredients together: cornmeal, flour, salt, sugar, baking powder, baking soda, and the peppers into a mixing bowl. Stir in the beaten eggs combined with the buttermilk, the fat, and onion.

　　Preheat oil to 365°F (185°C). If you are using a deep skillet, allow about 2 inches (5 cm) of fat for frying. Drop the batter by teaspoonfuls into the hot fat. The hushpuppies will sink to the bottom, rise to the top, and turn of their own accord as they cook. When golden brown, after a total cooking time of about 3 to 5 minutes, remove with a slotted spoon and drain on absorbent paper. Do not over-brown, as the hushpuppies will turn bitter. They can be held on brown paper in a warm oven for a few minutes, but serve as soon as possible.

Leftover corn bread is often crumbled into a large tumbler and covered with freshly churned ice-cold buttermilk. This makes a farm-style supper for the hottest summer nights and demands only the simplest accompaniment: sliced tomatoes, cucumbers and onions, maybe one-half of a ripe cantaloupe sprinkled with salt and pepper.

Yields 6 to 8 servings

Cracklings

2 to 3 ounces (60 to 85 g) pork
   sidemeat
1/4 cup (60 ml) cold water

Remove any rind from the sidemeat and dice finely. Combine the sidemeat with the water in the skillet over low heat. Cook, stirring occasionally, until the fat is rendered and the cracklings crisp and brown, approximately 40 minutes. Drain the cracklings on a brown paper bag. The rendered fat may be employed as the shortening for the corn bread, if desired.

The batter

1 1/2 cups (355 ml) yellow or white
   cornmeal
1 cup (122 g) flour
3 teaspoons baking powder
3/4 teaspoon baking soda
1 tablespoon sugar
1/2 teaspoon salt

1 1/2 cups (355 ml) buttermilk
3 eggs
4 tablespoons (60 g) melted
   butter, shortening, bacon fat,
   or rendered fat from cracklings
2 tablespoons cracklings

Recommended equipment: A 9-inch (22 1/2 cm) cake pan or 8-inch (20 cm) ovenproof iron skillet, brown paper bag.

Preheat oven to 425°F (218°C).
   Combine the cornmeal, flour, baking powder, baking soda, sugar, and salt and sift well. Beat the buttermilk and eggs together with 3 tablespoons of the melted fat.
   Brush the cake pan or skillet with the remaining melted fat and preheat it in the oven for 5 minutes. Combine the cracklings and the liquid and dry ingredients, and stir until just mixed. Pour into the hot

pan and bake 30 minutes in middle level of oven. When done, it will be golden brown and the cake will have pulled away from the sides of the pan.

ᥣ Spoon Bread ᥤ

Spoon bread is the most regal of all the cornmeal dishes and is part of many formal southern dinners. Its slight sweetness pairs well with pork and grilled game.

Yields 4 servings

1½ tablespoons (23 g) butter and
  2 tablespoons cornmeal
½ cup (61 g) flour
1 cup (235 ml) yellow cornmeal
½ teaspoon salt
1 tablespoon sugar

1 tablespoon (15 g) butter
1¼ cups (295 ml) boiling water
2 eggs, separated
1 cup (235 ml) buttermilk
1 teaspoon baking soda

Recommended equipment: A 2-quart (2 L) glass or ceramic soufflé dish, hand mixer.

Preheat oven to 325°F (163°C). Butter the soufflé dish with the 1½ tablespoons of butter and thoroughly coat the inside with the 2 tablespoons of cornmeal.

Combine the flour, cornmeal, salt, and sugar and sift into a mixing bowl. Add the butter to the boiling water and when melted, slowly pour into the meal mixture, stirring constantly. Allow to cool slightly and add the two egg yolks, well beaten. Beat the egg whites until stiff. Add the buttermilk and soda to the cornmeal batter and quickly fold in the egg whites. Pour into the soufflé dish and bake on middle rack of preheated oven for approximately 45 minutes. When done, the top should be brown, but the center should be slightly soft.

ᥣ Hominy Grits ᥤ

Both words, grits and hominy, with ancient origins from opposite sides of the Atlantic, were combined to describe one of the signature foods of the South. Grits comes from the Old English "grytt," which even in its earliest forms most often appeared as the plural, "grytta." It meant any bran or chaff, and implied coarsely ground grain. Oat grits are common in Scotland, though the first known written reference, by the great scholar Ælfric, referred to wheat, "hwæte gryttan."

In the southern United States, grits refers to the ground product of hominy. Hominy has had many suggested etymologies, all of which center around native American word combinations meaning parched corn. Roger Williams in 1643 suggested a derivation from the Algonquin "Appuminnéonash," meaning "he roasts grains." European settlers found hominy common throughout the corn-growing regions of North America and spelled it variously: homini, omine, homine, hommoney.

To produce hominy, dried corn is first soaked in an alkali solution to facilitate removal of the hulls. The East Coast Indians leached wood ashes to obtain lye. The natives farther west and through Central America relied on lime from limestone. After soaking, hominy can be cooked as a whole grain. The Mexican soup "pozole" is an authentic remnant of native hominy cooking. More often, in the southern United States, hominy is dried again and then ground for grits. In the Carolina coastal country, grist, which means grain to be ground, was confused early on with grits, the ground product. The result is one must read "grits" for "hominy" in Charleston and Beaufort cookbooks. Typically, the Charlestonian is quite secure in his malapropism and is quick to correct any outsider. Even the eminent American linguist Raven McDavid found he had something to learn on the subject: "In South Carolina I was taught that hominy designated what the less fortunate called grits."

Basic Boiled Grits

Modern processing has done little for grits. A long, slow cooking is necessary to produce the correct creamy consistency which is still punctuated by a slight pebbly contrast. Basic boiled grits are mostly breakfast food, best with country ham and fried eggs.

Yields 6 servings

4½ cups (1 L) water
1 teaspoon salt
1 cup (235 ml) hominy grits
Butter

Optional: ¼ cup to ¾ cup (60 to 180 ml) grated sharp Cheddar cheese

Recommended equipment: A 3-quart (3 L) heavy-bottomed saucepan, wire whisk.

Bring the salted water to a strong boil in the saucepan. Slowly sift the grits through one hand into the water while stirring with the whisk in the other hand. When all grits have been added, continue stirring and reduce the heat to low until only an occasional bubble breaks the surface. Continue cooking for 30 to 40 minutes, stirring frequently to prevent scorching. Beat in a good quantity of butter (and the optional cheese) if serving immediately or follow directions below for more elaborate preparations.

◟ Fried Grits ◞

Fried grits usually appear at the supper table to accompany any meat with a gravy.

Yields 6 servings

1 recipe Basic Boiled Grits (see
    page 30)
5 tablespoons (75 g) butter
1 egg, well beaten
3 tablespoons (45 g) butter or
    bacon fat

Recommended equipment: A loaf pan, wire whisk, 12-inch (30 cm) cast-iron skillet or enameled cast-iron sauté pan.

Grease the loaf pan with a nut of the butter. While the grits are still hot, beat in the remainder of the 5 tablespoons of butter. Quickly beat in the egg, taking care not to let it cook before it is completely incorporated. Pour grits into the loaf pan and let cool, covered loosely, at room temperature for 45 minutes. When cool, refrigerate for further use, or turn out (the grits will leave the pan surprisingly easily). Cut into ½ inch (1 cm) slices.

Melt the remaining butter or bacon fat in the skillet or sauté pan and fry over medium heat on each side for about 12 minutes until golden brown.

Biscuits and Bread

Grits Croquettes

As croquettes, grits can enter a more elaborate, formal meal as an unusual starchy accompaniment. They stand up well to such entrées as rack of lamb and veal kidneys.

Yields 6 servings

1 recipe Basic Boiled Grits (see page 30)
5 tablespoons (75 g) butter
2 eggs, well beaten
Lard or shortening for frying

Flour
1 egg, beaten, for dipping croquettes
Fine bread or cracker crumbs
1 bunch fresh parsley

Recommended equipment: A 12-inch (30 cm) cast-iron skillet or deep fryer, frying thermometer, slotted spoon, brown paper bag.

While the grits are still hot, beat in the 5 tablespoons of butter. Quickly beat in the two eggs, taking care not to let them cook before they are completely incorporated. Turn into a large bowl. When cool enough to handle, shape into ovals the size of a small egg. Using three separate shallow bowls or flat dishes, pour flour in one. Place an egg in the second bowl and beat it well. Add fine bread or cracker crumbs to the third.

In the skillet or deep fryer, bring the lard to 360°F (180°C). Roll the grits in flour, egg, and crumbs, and deep fry until golden brown.

Trim the stems of one bunch of the greenest, freshest parsley. Wash and dry *well;* carefully fry the parsley until crisp in deep fat (approximately 15 to 20 seconds). Drain well on brown paper bag and use as garnish for croquettes.

Awendaw

Awendaw is a descendant of native American cooking, taking its name from an ancient Indian settlement outside of Charleston, South Carolina.

Yields 4 to 6 servings

2 cups (475 ml) water
3/4 teaspoon salt
7 tablespoons grits
4 tablespoons (60 g) butter

1½ cups (355 ml) milk
1 cup (235 ml) yellow cornmeal
3 eggs
Butter and cornmeal for pan

Biscuits and Bread

Recommended equipment: A loaf pan and brown paper, 1½-quart (1½ L) saucepan with lid, medium mixing bowl.

Line the bottom of the pan with brown paper. Grease it and the sides of the pan well with butter. Dust the interior with a small amount of cornmeal.

Bring the water to a rapid boil in a saucepan and stir in the grits and salt. Cook over medium heat for 25 minutes, stirring frequently. Beat in the butter when grits are done and remove from heat. In the meantime combine the milk and cornmeal in a mixing bowl and let stand at least 15 minutes. Preheat oven to 350°F (177°C).

Stir the slightly cooled grits into the cornmeal mixture and beat the eggs in, one by one. When well mixed, pour batter into loaf pan and bake in middle level of preheated oven for approximately 50 minutes. Serve hot with plenty of butter, or, if leftover, lightly toasted or fried in butter.

Biscuits

The biscuit has changed during the centuries, both in spelling and preparation. As soon as I had learned to spell this word, I wanted another, more logical pronunciation. Bis-quit´seemed apt. Eventually, I found my way to the *Oxford English Dictionary.* It takes little pleasure in the affectations of the past two centuries: "The regular form in Eng. from 16th to 18th c. was *bisket,* as still pronounced; the current *biscuit* is a senseless adoption of the mod. French spelling, without the Fr. pronunciation." Matters could be worse: besquite, bysqwyte, byscute are all historical antecedents.

The biscuit of these latter spellings was the movable feast of armies and navies: "Armour thei had plente, & god besquite to mete," reported Brunne in his *Chronicles,* 1330. The biscuit traveled well because it was exactly what its name implied: twice baked; any crisp, dry flat bread (our crackers) of England or France is still a biscuit, biscotte. Of all modern forms of the southern biscuit, the beaten biscuit most nearly resembles its hard-baked ancestors. Stored in airtight tins, it lasts for weeks.

Raised biscuits were originally leavened by a natural or induced fermentation. The rapidity and reliability of raising the dough by chemical means later established the preeminence of the baking powder biscuit. Untrusting cooks combined both methods to ensure success and created such hybrid recipes as angel or bride's biscuits.

For tender biscuits, do not overmix the ingredients, especially after the liquid is added. You will knead slightly, however, to give this unsupported dough enough stretched gluten to maintain its shape and height. The French call this gentle stretching "fraisage" and apply it to various short pastes (pâtes) used for tart shells, and so forth. Too much exertion, though, will result in lower volume and increased density. When cutting the dough, use a clean, sharp edge, dipped in plain flour. A dull or dirty edge will pinch top to bottom, sealing the edges and preventing proper rise. Twisting the cutter will effect the same damage. Extra leavening will not compensate for lack of technique: in excess, baking powder tastes bitter and discolors the finished product.

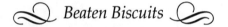 *Beaten Biscuits*

Beaten biscuits are a symbol of the Old South, when time and labor weren't luxuries but a way of life. They still appear at fancy parties, and especially weddings, sandwiched with wafer-thin country ham. At such events, they rarely exceed a 1¼ inch diameter.

Yields about 5 to 6 dozen, depending upon size

4 cups (488 g) flour
¾ teaspoon salt
2 teaspoons sugar
3 tablespoons (45 g) lard

1 cup (235 ml) cold water
1½ tablespoons (23 g) melted
    butter

Recommended equipment: A medium mixing bowl; blending fork; wooden spoon; mallet, cleaver, or rolling pin; 1-inch (2½ cm) biscuit cutter (the size of a doughnut hole); baking sheet.

Sift the flour, salt, and sugar together. With the fingertips or blending fork, work the lard into the flour until the fat is completely and evenly dispersed. Make a well in the center of the mixture, add the water all at once, and stir with the wooden spoon until it is well mixed. Turn out and knead until dough is smooth, approximately 25 strokes.

Preheat oven to 325°F (163°C). Using 10 strokes at a time, begin beating the dough with a mallet, cleaver, or rolling pin into a rectangle approximately 15 by 6 inches (38 × 15 cm). Fold the rectangle into thirds, turn 90 degrees to the right, and repeat. Do this at least 30 times (300 strokes, 500 for company). Roll out to a ½ inch (1¼ cm) thickness and cut with a cutter dipped in flour. Place on an ungreased baking sheet and brush the tops with melted butter.

Prick with a fork and bake in preheated oven for 20 minutes, then raise heat to 350°F (177°C) and bake 10 minutes until slightly browned.

⤫ Raised Biscuits ⤬

Unlike most regional foods, biscuits have become increasingly popular in the twentieth century and have been adopted with great success by fast-food restaurants, some of which do a creditable job with the southern standby. There is probably no easier way to provide a good, homebaked bread for any meal. In Kentucky and Tennessee, the raw, cut dough is often fried in hot fat to accompany fried chicken.

Yields 16 biscuits

2 cups (244 g) all purpose flour	1 tablespoon (15 g) lard, chilled
3¼ teaspoons baking powder	2 tablespoons (30 g) butter,
½ teaspoon salt	chilled
1 teaspoon sugar	¾ cup (180 ml) cold milk
2 tablespoons (30 g) vegetable	Flour for working surface
shortening, chilled	

Recommended equipment: A baking sheet, medium mixing bowl, blending fork or pastry blender, 2¼-inch (5¾ cm) biscuit cutter.

Preheat oven to 425°F (218°C).

Sift the flour, baking powder, salt, and sugar together into a mixing bowl. Cut in the cold fats with a pastry blender, blending fork, or the fingertips. Add the cold milk and stir quickly, using 10 to 12 strokes. Turn the dough out onto a floured surface. Sprinkle with a small amount of flour and knead lightly, 6 to 12 strokes. Push the dough out and fold back on itself each fourth stroke. Pat out or roll out to a thickness of ¾ inch (2 cm). Using a 2¼-inch (5¾ cm) cutter dipped in flour, cut the dough and place the biscuits close together (but not touching) on the ungreased baking sheet. Bake for 12 to 15 minutes until risen and lightly browned.

❧ *Angel or Bride's Biscuits* ❧

Yields 16 to 20 biscuits

1 cup (235 ml) buttermilk
1 package dry yeast (¼ ounce or
 7 g)
2½ cups (306 g) flour
1 teaspoon baking soda
1 teaspoon salt
1 teaspoon sugar

¼ cup (60 ml) vegetable
 shortening, chilled
¼ cup (60 ml) butter, chilled
Flour for kneading and rolling
2 tablespoons (30 g) butter,
 melted

Recommended equipment: A small saucepan, medium mixing bowl, 2¼-inch (5¾ cm) biscuit cutter.

Heat the buttermilk to lukewarm, remove from heat, and stir in yeast to dissolve. Meanwhile, sift flour with baking soda, salt, and sugar. Cut the vegetable shortening and butter into the flour mixture until it resembles coarse meal. Refrigerate.

When buttermilk and yeast are at room temperature, beat the liquid into the flour mixture with 10 to 20 quick strokes. Refrigerate again for 10 minutes.

Sprinkle a counter or pastry marble with flour, turn the dough onto it, and knead 15 to 20 strokes, until the dough just coalesces. Add flour when kneading if necessary (especially in humid weather). Pat out to a ½ inch (1¼ cm) thickness and cut with a biscuit cutter. Dip both sides of the biscuit in melted butter and place on an ungreased baking sheet. Let rise in a warm, draft-free place until doubled in volume.

Preheat oven to 400°F (204°C). Bake for 10 to 12 minutes on middle level of oven until golden brown.

❧ *Sally Lunn Bread* ❧

Tucked away on some cozy lane of Bath, England, lies the birthplace of a bread which became a mad fad of the eighteenth century. There, a tea-shop proprietress, Sally Lunn, secured immortality for her name and the bread which she offered to her increasingly fashionable customers as the rich and titled occupied the tiny resort to take the waters. Or so goes the apocryphal history—unfortunately no historical record exists of the lady or her shop. A more academic, but equally undocumented, explanation proposes Sally Lunn as a corruption of "sol-imeme," the name of a similar French bread from Alsace. Whatever its shady background, it became one of the most popular yeast breads of the South.

A vigorous hand beating is required to exercise the gluten, hence the stroke counts in the following recipe. The limited rotary action of a mixer or food processor cannot give the elastic stretch that you achieve through long and high strokes. Kneading a dough this soft would necessitate the incorporation of too much flour; the lovely brioche-like texture would be destroyed.

Yields 10 to 12 servings

1 cup (235 ml) milk	3 eggs, well beaten
½ cup (115 g) butter	4 cups (488 g) flour
¼ cup (50 g) sugar	1 teaspoon salt
1 package dry yeast (¼ ounce or 7 g)	2 tablespoons (30 g) butter

Recommended equipment: A 9- or 10-inch (22½ or 25 cm) tube pan, 1½-quart (1½ L) stainless steel or enameled saucepan, large mixing bowl, wooden spoon.

Combine the milk, butter, and sugar in the saucepan over gentle heat and stir until butter and sugar dissolve. Let cool to lukewarm and add yeast to dissolve. Let rest until yeast bubbles. Stir in the 3 beaten eggs and turn mixture into the bowl.

Sift the flour and salt together and add all at once to the liquid in the bowl. Beat vigorously with the wooden spoon, counting 400 strokes. Dough should become elastic and somewhat shiny. If not, beat harder and longer. Then cover the bowl with a damp towel or plastic wrap, set in a warm, draft-free place, and let rise until double in volume. Beat down with the wooden spoon, counting 50 strokes, and set aside for 15 minutes.

With the 2 tablespoons of butter, grease the tube pan well. Beat the dough again for 50 strokes and pour into the tube pan. Cover and let rise until doubled again in volume.

Preheat oven to 375°F (190°C). Bake in middle level of the oven for approximately 40 minutes until the bread is golden brown and has pulled away from the edge of the pan.

⤳ Moravian Sugar Bread and Love Feast Coffee ⤳

The Anglican Church sent Charles Woodmason on a mission to the Carolina upland in 1766. He found little to his liking, especially in the larders, as he related in his diaries, published as *The Carolina Back Country on the Eve of the Revolution:* "Nothing but Indian Corn Meal to be had Bacon and Eggs in some Places—No Butter, Rice, or Milk—As for Tea and Coffee they know it not. These people are all from Ireland, and live wholly on Buttermilk, Clabber and what in England is given to the Hogs and Dogs." Only among the Moravian settlements in North Carolina could he find anything praiseworthy, and he provides an exuberant description:

The Spot is not only Rich, fertile, and luxuriant, but the most Romantic in Nature Sir Phillip Sydneys Description of Arcadia, falls short of this *real* Arcadia Georgia, Circassia, Armenia, or whatever Region it may be compared too. . . . Here they have laid out two Towns—Bethlehem and Bethsada; delightfully charming! Rocks, Cascades, Hills, Vales, Groves, Plains—Woods, Waters all most strangely intermixt, so that Imagination cannot paint anything more vivid. They have Mills, Furnaces, Forges, Potteries, Founderies All Trades, and all things in and among themselves . . . they are all *Bees,* not a Drone suffer'd in the Hive.

The Moravians celebrated their religion in every aspect of their lives. The beginning or end of most projects—a new building, a successful harvest—was marked by the religious ritual called the love feast. Hymns were sung and a simple communal meal of bread and coffee was served.

The bread

Yields 16 servings

1 package dry yeast
½ cup (118 ml) warm water
1 cup (235 ml) milk
½ cup (101 g) granulated sugar
1½ teaspoons salt
½ cup (115 g) butter
2 eggs, slightly beaten
5½ cups (671 g) flour

½ cup (115 g) butter
1 pound (450 g) light brown sugar
1 teaspoon powdered cinnamon
¾ teaspoon freshly grated nutmeg
Butter for greasing pans

Recommended equipment: A 1½-quart (1½ L) saucepan, two large bowls, two baking dishes (see pages 191–92).

Dissolve the yeast in the warm water. Combine the milk, granulated sugar, salt, and butter in a saucepan, heating gently until the sugar dissolves and the butter is melted. Remove saucepan from heat and cool slightly. Stir in dissolved yeast and beaten eggs. Transfer mixture to a large bowl, and gradually add the flour, stirring constantly. Turn out the dough onto a floured surface and knead it until smooth. Butter or grease a large mixing bowl and place the dough into it, turning it over once. Cover with a damp towel and let rise in a warm, draft-free place until volume doubles.

Punch dough down and divide in two, spreading one half in each of the baking dishes. Brush surfaces with a little butter, and let rise until volume doubles.

Preheat oven to 375°F (190°C). Make holes in dough by poking it with a finger. (Moravian wisdom has it that a miserly cook uses her index finger, the generous one her thumb.)

Melt the ½ cup butter with the light brown sugar, cinnamon, and nutmeg. Pour over the dough, filling the indentations. Bake about 25 minutes. Serve warm.

The coffee

For the love feast the Congregation Council of the church had sanctified coffee rather than tea in 1789, but suggested sangaree for the hot weather in August. The Moravians shared with all their neighbors this penchant for coffee. In times of scarcity, southerners sought substitutes wherever they could find them: grains, sweet potatoes, acorns, and the seeds of persimmons, okra, and watermelon. In good times, though, each day's coffee was roasted in the morning, kitchens filling with the aroma.

It's a satisfying step backwards to roast coffee in a skillet on top of the stove. Beans should rest in a single layer and cook over a medium high heat. It is imperative to keep the beans moving to avoid scorched areas. Some beans turn much more quickly than others; this is not a problem unless scorching does occur. In 10 minutes, I have a pan full of richly roasted beans. When I started roasting my own beans it was helpful to have a few whole beans already roasted to my taste for comparison. Now I can judge by the odor alone. Roasted beans should cool off the fire uncovered and should be stored in airtight containers.

Grinding can be done by hand or in an electric coffee grinder. A blender will work, but gives a slightly uneven grind.

Yields 30 to 40 servings

2 gallons (7 L) water
1 pound (450 g) dark, freshly
   roasted finely ground coffee

(such as French Roast or
  Espresso)
2 cups (403 g) sugar
2½ cups (590 ml) half-and-half

Recommended equipment: An unbleached, undyed muslin bag approximately 8 by 8 inches (20 × 20 cm); needle and thread; an 8-quart (8 L) stainless steel stockpot.

Fill the clean cloth bag with the coffee and sew securely. Bring the water to a boil and add the coffee. Keep at a simmer, but not a boil, for 12 to 15 minutes. Remove the bag, add sugar and cream, and serve immediately.

A note on the coffee bag: Use clean, unbleached muslin. Wash several times with no soap. A bag 8 × 8 inches (20 × 20 cm) will hold 1 pound of coffee. If you want to reuse the bag, add stainless steel snaps for closing, but never use soap in washing the sack.

Rice

Now hopping-john was F. Jasmine's very favorite food. She had always warned them to wave a plate of rice and peas before her nose when she was in her coffin, to make certain there was no mistake; for if a breath of life was left in her, she would sit up and eat, but if she smelled the hopping-john, and did not stir, then they could just nail down the coffin and be certain she was truly dead.

Carson McCullers, *The Member of the Wedding*

Once, when one ordered the finest rice obtainable, Carolina Gold, the pride of Charleston and Savannah, was the only answer. It was the preferred rice of England and the Continent; it was demanded by Oriental princes. Today, ironically, the grain sold as Carolina rice is likely to be grown in Louisiana and Arkansas. Both political and natural history helped end the east coast domination of the crop; by the early twentieth century rice belonged to the Mississippi valley.

In the late seventeenth century, however, Britain looked to its North American colonies to help break its dependence on the European Continent. Practically unable to support its dense population and geographically unsuited to produce its luxury foods, Britain depended on France and the Iberian peninsula for such foods as wine and oil. Despite great expectations for the southern colonies of North America, the cultivation of the grape and olive failed. Rice proved the exception that unexpectedly helped Britain break the Continental hold on the food trade. Sometime shortly before 1686, the gold seed rice, obtained from Madagascar, was planted by Dr. Henry Woodward in Charleston. By 1700 there were not enough ships in Charleston to export the crop. The wealth derived from rice was already building the dazzling cosmopolitan status of that city and its planters.

For two centuries rice was supreme among the crops raised from Wilmington, North Carolina, to the Florida boundary. The east coast plantations were elaborate hydraulic machines (fueled mainly by the manual labor of black slaves) that flooded fields with fresh water and checked the rise of salt water. At the end of the Civil War, with slavery abolished and the economy ruined, the system began to break down. Money, as a commodity, was not available to pay manual workers in any labor-intensive field. In the 1880s, just as the rice economy began to recover, a series of storms culminated in a great hurricane. Salt water inundated the fields, the entire crop was lost, and the industry foundered. Louisiana was the beneficiary. By 1901 the *New Orleans Picayune* could boast: "The cultivation of rice began in Louisiana nearly a hundred years after it commenced in Georgia and South Carolina, but Louisiana now produces more of this beautiful grain than both these states combined." Because the fields of Louisiana were easily cultivated by machine, the manual laborers on the east coast were soon looking for jobs in timber and other industries.

In Louisiana, rice achieved its American culinary apotheosis. In a great variety of jambalayas, it became the central element around which a number of complex combinations were arranged. Rice was no longer a bland foil for setting off exotic flavors but the featured item absorbing, reacting with, and defining other ingredients.

⟋ Hoppin' John ⟍

Southerners may make resolutions for the New Year, but they know success (or lack of it) depends more on what is eaten on 1 January than on all the good intentions in the world. More black-eyed peas and collards are consumed on that day than any other time of the year—part of an antique gastronomic insurance policy. Collards are for a steady supply of folding green in the coming year; black-eyed peas for plenty of pocket change. Hoppin' John is a sort of jambalaya with a light touch. Do not stew the different elements into a homogeneous mush. Each pea, grain of rice, chunk of tomato, and piece of scallion should retain its individual identity, flavor, and texture.

Yields 4 to 6 servings

2 cups (475 ml) cooked Black-eyed Peas (see pages 66–67)
2 cups (475 ml) cooked rice
1 cup (235 ml) chopped fresh tomato
½ cup (118 ml) finely chopped scallions

½ teaspoon salt
¼ teaspoon freshly ground black pepper
Cheddar cheese, grated (optional)

Recommended equipment: A 12-inch (30 cm) cast-iron skillet or enameled cast-iron sauté pan with cover.

Heat the peas and rice separately if cold. (Add 3 tablespoons water to cold rice, cover, and steam briefly.) Combine lightly in the skillet or sauté pan, sprinkle the chopped tomato and scallions over all, and season with salt and pepper. Cover and heat through. Add grated cheddar cheese when serving, if desired.

Rice Croquettes

When serving rice croquettes, and any fried foods, remember they must be served immediately. These are especially good with country ham and all seafood, baked or poached.

Yields 4 servings

1½ cups (355 ml) cold, well-cooked rice

½ cup (61 g) flour

2 eggs, well beaten

½ teaspoon Tabasco sauce

½ cup (118 ml) sharp white Cheddar cheese, grated

Salt

⅛ teaspoon white pepper

Vegetable oil for deep frying

½ cup (118 ml) dry white bread crumbs

Recommended equipment: A medium mixing bowl, 12-inch (30 cm) cast-iron skillet or deep fryer, frying thermometer, slotted spoon, brown paper bag.

Sprinkle the flour over the cold, cooked rice in the mixing bowl and fold together gently. Beat the eggs with the Tabasco and add to the rice mixture. Fold in cheese, taste for salt, and season with white pepper. Let stand at room temperature for 20 minutes or refrigerate if not to be used immediately. Form into desired shapes, whether balls, cylinders, ovals, or any others, being careful not to exceed a diameter of 1½ inches (3¾ cm).

When ready to cook, pour oil in the skillet or deep fryer to a minimum depth of 2½ inches (6¼ cm) and heat it to 360°F (182°C). Roll the shaped croquettes in bread crumbs and fry until golden brown, about 2 minutes. Remove with slotted spoon, drain well on brown paper bag, and serve.

Rice Bread, Philpy

Philpy is just one of many rice breads prepared in the South. I once thought these breads confined to the Georgetown, South Carolina–Savannah, Georgia, region, but they were popular beyond the rice growing areas. Francisco de Mirada found the rice "tortillas" of Beaufort, North Carolina, delicious in the 1780s. *The Carolina Housewife* enjoyed a widespread distribution upon its publication in 1847, and its more than thirty recipes for rice breads could not have been passed over. *The Southern Agriculturist,* a well-respected and widely distributed journal, encouraged its readers to try submitted recipes for these breads. Philpy is one of the oldest named rice breads I have found. Recipes are still published for it in local South Carolina cookbooks, but I have yet to find a cook who still prepares it, or any other rice bread, regularly. It is a quick bread, much like corn bread, to accompany breakfast, lunch, or dinner.

Yields 4 servings

¾ cup (180 ml) well-cooked rice	½ teaspoon salt
½ cup (118 ml) buttermilk	½ teaspoon baking powder
1 egg, well beaten	½ teaspoon baking soda
1 cup (122 g) flour	Butter for greasing the pan

Recommended equipment: A medium mixing bowl, potato masher or ricer, rubber spatula, 9-inch (22½ cm) cake pan.

Preheat oven to 450°F (232°C). Grease the cake pan well and set aside.

Mash the cooked rice well in the bottom of the mixing bowl. Slowly add the buttermilk while continuing to mash the rice. Stir in the beaten egg. Sift the flour with the salt, baking powder, and baking soda. Fold the dry ingredients into the liquid and pour into the greased cake pan. Bake on the middle level of the preheated oven for about 30 minutes or until lightly golden. Serve very hot with much butter.

Rice Omelet

The rice omelet will remind many of an Italian *frittata* in its double cooking. Initially, the eggs set up in a skillet, over a burner. They are then finished off in the oven, where an intense blast of heat puffs the beaten whites to a soufflé-like consistency. The base may be prepared ahead of time with the whites folded in just before cooking. Chopped ham or bacon, bits of roast, or cooked shellfish may be added to make a more substantial dish. A tomato, mornay, or hollandaise sauce may be poured over the omelet at the table; the Cajun Tomato Sauce (see page 147) also contrasts dramatically with the eggs.

Yields 4 servings for a light luncheon entrée, or first course

1 cup (235 ml) well-cooked rice
1/3 cup (80 ml) whole milk
4 eggs
1/4 cup (60 ml) finely chopped
 scallions
1/4 cup (60 ml) finely chopped
 mushrooms
1/2 cup (118 ml) sharp white
 Cheddar cheese, grated

1 tablespoon chopped fresh basil
 (or 1 teaspoon dried)
1 tablespoon chopped fresh
 parsley
1/8 teaspoon (or more) Tabasco
 sauce
2 tablespoons (30 g) butter
1/4 teaspoon salt

Recommended equipment: A 1½-quart (1½ L) saucepan with lid, two mixing bowls, wire whisk or electric mixer, ovenproof 12-inch (30 cm) cast-iron skillet or enameled cast-iron sauté pan, rubber spatula.

Preheat oven to 400°F (204°C) and set a rack at the middle level.

Combine the cooked rice and the milk in the saucepan; heat, covered, over medium heat until the rice absorbs most of the liquid and let cool. Separate the eggs, reserving the whites to be beaten stiffly later. Beat the yolks well and combine with the rice. Add the scallions, mushrooms, and cheese. Season with the herbs and Tabasco.

Melt the butter in the skillet or sauté pan over medium heat. Working quickly, and in a clean bowl with clean beaters, beat the whites with the salt until stiff peaks form and fold them gently but thoroughly into the egg yolk mixture. Pour the eggs into the skillet and cook gently for about 3 minutes, or until the sides and bottom of the omelet are set. The interior should still be liquid at this point. Run the skillet into the middle level of the preheated oven, and cook the omelet until well puffed and slightly browned. This should take between 5 and 6 minutes. When done cut the omelet into wedges to serve and do so from the skillet at the table.

Charleston Purloos

I interviewed several Charlestonians on the subject of purloo. My first question was, "How do you spell purloo?" The answers were: purloo, perloo, perlo, perlau, pilau, and pilaf. I was assured that if I could think of another way to spell it, that would be fine as well. All Charles tonians pronounce it the same, however, no matter what the spelling: per-lō. Purloo is also the single dish of traditional Charleston fare that all informants—black and white, above and below Broad Street—recognized immediately.

Bacon, onion, sweet green pepper, tomatoes, and rice—these are the ingredients of the basic purloo form, also known as red rice. This is much what many Americans call Spanish rice; in Charleston, Spanish rice is *green* rice, full of parsley and bell pepper. Red rice often accompanies fried chicken or fried fish with coleslaw. Charlestonians also recommend it served cold or at room temperature and for picnicking on the banks of the Ashley River or by the surf on Sullivan's Island. Many variations are played on the theme; two more substantial versions follow. Sometimes rice is cooked (that is, steamed) separately from the flavorings. Other times it is combined raw with the other ingredients and baked. One Charlestonian told me: "I reckon if it has rice in it, it's purloo."

ᴖᴗ Chicken Purloo ᴖᴗ

Yields 6 to 8 servings

1 chicken weighing about 4 pounds (1800 g), poached (see page 114)
3 cups (705 ml) stock from poaching
6 slices of bacon (approximately 5 ounces or 140 g)
2½ cups (590 ml) chopped onion
¾ cup (180 ml) chopped celery
¾ cup (180 ml) chopped, peeled carrot
3 garlic cloves, chopped
3 tablespoons flour
1 14-ounce (400 g) can whole Italian tomatoes, drained and chopped

1 teaspoon dried thyme
¼ teaspoon dried basil
¼ to ½ teaspoon dried red pepper flakes
½ ounce (15 g) dried French cèpes or Italian porcini, chopped
Salt and freshly ground black pepper
2 ounces (60 g) cold butter
1½ tablespoons chopped fresh parsley
6 cups (1410 ml) hot, cooked rice

Recommended equipment: A Dutch oven.

Bone, skin, and chop the chicken into regular pieces ¾ inch by 1¼ inches (2 × 3 cm). Chop the bacon and render in the Dutch oven, cooking slowly until it browns at the edge; do not let it become crisp. Add onion, celery, carrot, and garlic and continue cooking until vegetables are tender. Add flour and cook, stirring constantly until the flour browns lightly. Pour in stock and tomatoes with the chicken, thyme, basil, red pepper flakes, and chopped mushrooms. Bring to a simmer, taste for salt and pepper, and cook for 30 minutes.

Before serving, stir in the fresh parsley and the butter, one tablespoon at a time. Serve over hot rice.

Okra and Ham Purloo

Yields 4 servings

3 slices bacon (approximately 2½ ounces or 70 g)

1 cup (235 ml) chopped onion

½ cup (118 ml) chopped green bell pepper

1 cup (235 ml) thinly sliced okra

1 garlic clove, chopped

8 ounces (225 g) country ham, cut into matchstick shapes 1 by ¼ by ¼ inch (2½ × ⅔ × ⅔ cm)

1 cup (235 ml) eggplant, peeled and cubed

1 14-ounce (400 g) can whole Italian tomatoes, chopped, with juice

1 teaspoon dried thyme

½ teaspoon dried basil

⅛ teaspoon red pepper flakes

1 cup (235 ml) raw long grain rice

2 cups (475 ml) water

Recommended equipment: A 12-inch (30 cm) cast-iron skillet or Dutch oven.

Preheat oven to 400°F (204°C).

Chop the bacon and render it over medium heat in the skillet or Dutch oven until it browns at the edges, but is not crisp. Stir in onion, pepper, and okra and sauté until just wilted. Add garlic, ham, and eggplant and continue cooking for about 5 more minutes. Add tomatoes, thyme, basil, red pepper flakes, rice, and water. Bring to a boil over high heat. Shake the pan well to distribute the ingredients evenly and place on the middle level of the preheated oven. Immediately reduce heat to 325°F (163°C) and bake for 30 minutes or until rice is tender. Serve as a main dish, not as an accompaniment.

Rice

Red Beans and Rice

New Orleans natives hold red beans and rice closer to their hearts than any other of their many fabled dishes—so much so that Louis Armstrong made his autograph "Red beans and ricely yours." After Mardi Gras, the andouille—a local smoked pork sausage—and ham are omitted for the duration of Lent. Red beans are, if anything, even more popular then.

Yields 8 to 10 servings

1 pound (450 g) dried red kidney
   beans
2 quarts (2 L) cold water for
   soaking the beans

Sauce and seasonings for the beans

1 cup (235 ml) chopped onion
1 cup (235 ml) chopped green
   bell pepper
1 cup (235 ml) chopped celery
4 garlic cloves, minced
4 tablespoons (60 g) bacon fat or
   lard
1 14-ounce (400 g) can tomatoes

5 to 7 cups (1185 to 1655 ml) cold
   water
3/4 teaspoon dried red pepper
   flakes
1 teaspoon dried thyme
1 bay leaf
1 smoked ham hock

The meats

2 tablespoons (30 g) bacon fat or
   lard
4 ounces (115 g) boiled ham cut
   into 1/2 inch (1 cm) cubes

2 pounds (900 g) andouille or any
   hot smoked sausage, sliced 3/8
   inch (1 cm) thick

The rice

2 1/2 cups (590 ml) raw long grain
   rice
4 1/2 cups (1 L) water
1 1/2 teaspoons salt
4 tablespoons (60 g) butter

Rice

Final seasonings

Salt
Freshly ground black pepper
Tabasco sauce
¼ cup (60 ml) fresh, chopped
   parsley

Recommended equipment: An 8-quart (8 L) stockpot, 12-inch (30 cm) cast-iron skillet or enameled cast-iron sauté pan, 1½-quart (1½ L) saucepan with lid.

Pick through the dried beans, removing any defective beans or debris. Cover with cold water and soak overnight.

   Melt the 4 tablespoons of fat in the stockpot, and sauté the onion, green pepper, celery, and garlic over medium high heat. Drain the tomatoes, reserving the juice. Chop and add them, along with their juice and the 5 to 7 cups of water, to the stockpot.

   Drain the beans, rinse thoroughly under cold water, and add to the stockpot. Add the red pepper flakes, thyme, bay, and ham hock. Bring to a boil, reduce heat and simmer 1½ hours, adding more water if necessary.

   Heat the two tablespoons of fat in the skillet or sauté pan and brown the cubed ham and sliced sausages. Add to the beans, stirring in very gently. Simmer for 20 more minutes or until beans are tender, but not mushy. Taste for salt, pepper, and Tabasco.

   Prepare rice by bringing water to a boil, then add the rice and salt. Cover and cook over low heat about 25 minutes. Remove from heat and keep covered.

   Before serving, stir the fresh parsley into the beans, and fold the butter into the hot rice. Present the beans and rice separately at the table, each diner establishing the desired proportions.

 Green Rice

In southern cooking plain boiled rice is often spiked with herbs and scallions when it is used as a foil for robust dishes such as Creole sauces, red beans and rice, and gumbos. The greens create interesting contrasts with the rice but do not interfere with the well-developed flavors of well-simmered sauces.

Rice

3¹/₄ cups (765 ml) water
1¹/₂ cups (350 ml) long grain rice
¹/₂ teaspoon salt
4 tablespoons butter

4 tablespoons fresh, chopped
   parsley
4 tablespoons thinly sliced
   scallions, white and green
   parts

Recommended equipment: A medium saucepan with lid.

Bring the water to a hard boil, add rice and salt, cover, and cook over low heat about 20 minutes. The rice should be fully cooked, tender, and dry.

Scatter the butter, parsley and scallions over the rice. Carefully fork the seasonings through the rice. Cover the pot again and let sit 5 minutes before serving.

Duck and Sausage Jambalaya

Jambalaya is identified today as Cajun French food in the popular mind, but historically it is a gift from the Spanish rule of New Orleans. Like gumbos, jambalayas often contain a variety of seafood from the Gulf of Mexico. Duck, though, is a great feature of Louisiana cooking, and the following recipe incorporates both that fowl and the hot smoky Cajun sausage andouille.

Yields 8 to 10 servings

The meats

1 duck weighing about 4¹/₂
   pounds (2 kg), preferably fresh
Salt and freshly ground black
   pepper

1 pound (450 g) andouille or any
   hot smoked sausage
4 ounces (115 g) boiled ham
Duck giblets: heart, liver, and
   gizzard

The aromatic vegetables

2 green bell peppers, chopped
1 cup (235 ml) chopped celery
1½ (355 ml) cups chopped onion

4 garlic cloves, peeled and
  chopped
3 tablespoons (45 g) lard or bacon
  fat

The broth

1 35-ounce (990 g) can whole
  tomatoes
4 cups (1 L) chicken stock or
  water
3 teaspoons salt
1 teaspoon freshly ground black
  pepper
1 teaspoon Tabasco sauce

2 teaspoons dried basil
1 teaspoon dried thyme
2 bay leaves
2 tablespoons (30 g) lard or bacon
  fat
2½ cups (590 ml) raw long grain
  rice

Recommended equipment: A heavy roasting pan with rack, poultry shears, Dutch oven, 3-quart (3 L) saucepan.

Preheat oven to 425°F (218°C). Remove the giblets and wash the duck well. Split it down the backbone with either shears or a sharp boning knife. Flatten it slightly by cracking the ribs and pressing down on the septum. Sprinkle with salt and pepper and place it skin side up on a rack above a roasting pan or baking sheet (with sides to contain the grease). Poke the skin all over in the fatty areas to yield excess fat while cooking and roast for about 1 hour on the upper level of the oven or until juices run clear from the thigh. If unsure, err on the side of undercooking.

While duck is roasting continue with other preparations. Slice the sausage and dice the ham and giblets, setting aside for later use.

Chop the peppers, celery, onions, and garlic. Melt the 3 table-spoons of fat in the Dutch oven and sauté the vegetables over low heat until tender. Reserve in a bowl.

Drain the tomatoes, reserving the juice, and chop them. Combine them with the juice, chicken stock (or water), salt, pepper, Tabasco, basil, thyme, and bay in a saucepan and simmer for 20 minutes.

Sauté the rice in the 2 tablespoons of fat in the Dutch oven until just barely browned. Do not overcook or allow to pop. Reserve in a bowl.

When duck is done, remove to cool. Using 3 tablespoons of ren-

Rice

dered duck fat from the pan, brown the sausage, ham, and giblets in the Dutch oven. Remove with a slotted spoon and reserve.

Carefully remove excess grease from the roasting pan, taking care to leave behind any rendered juice or browned bits from the duck. Add these to the tomato mixture. When the duck is cool enough to handle, remove all meat from the bones (with skin intact) and chop it roughly.

Preheat the oven to 350°F (177°C). You are now ready to assemble the Jambalaya.

Scatter the sautéed vegetables over the bottom of the Dutch oven. Add the browned rice, distributing it evenly. Next add the meats: sausage slices, giblets, ham, and duck. Over all pour the hot tomato mixture. Cover tightly with a lid (or aluminum foil) and bake for 1 hour. The liquid should be absorbed and the rice thoroughly cooked.

Vegetables

At the mid-day meal, they ate heavily: a huge hot roast of beef, fat buttered lima-beans, tender corn smoking on the cob, thick red slabs of sliced tomatoes, rough savory spinach, hot yellow corn-bread, flaky biscuits, a deep-dish peach and apple cobbler spiced with cinnamon, tender cabbage, deep glass dishes piled with preserved fruits—cherries, pears, peaches.

Thomas Wolfe, *Look Homeward, Angel*

By July, it seems every rural family in the South must have its own roadside produce stand. Hand-painted signs—some of which have found their way into folk art galleries all over the country—announce peaches, tomatoes, watermelons, okra, onions, potatoes, corn by variety (Silver Queen is a current favorite), and cantaloupes under enough variant spellings to confound Dr. Johnson (my favorite: "can'telope"). And every stand has its loyal adherents. Even the efficiency of interstate travel is deserted for the back-road rewards of produce shopping. Motor trips to the mountains or shore necessitate stops that have grown into traditions, a respectful annual call for knowledgeable purchases: "They have good corn here." "No, let's wait to get beans at that stand on down the road."

Throughout the growing season, other farms open for pick-your-own harvests. It is almost mythical—a garden only for picking—no plowing, no weeding, no worry about frost or drought. City dwellers cannot resist the call of the canner—their eyes grow wide and wild as they imagine full pantries, buckling shelves, jars packed with the summer's multicolored gifts. Yet in the evening, after dinner, the baskets of peas gathered so enthusiastically in hunger seem bottomless.

Growing up, I used to think that television must have been invented solely to pass the time for pea shellers. Now when I go to the Carrboro Farmers' Market, I almost blush at the luxury of beans and peas for sale—already shelled!

A southerner's insistence on the finest, freshest vegetables comes naturally—almost everyone had a garden, or at least access to one (I know lawyers who are still paid in produce). City dwellers had reliable farmers who called at home early each morning with dew-laden pickings. One had a vegetable man, period, though the best were hard to come by. A farmer would check and cross-check the references of any potential customer. Those who proudly sold to the Sartorises did not call on the Snopeses. One's social standing could be accurately charted by knowing from whom one bought one's produce.

B.C.C. (or Before Climate Control), you might as well have gardened, for it was just as hot inside as out. Now it's a lot harder to convince yourself that it's truly worth the venture out when the temperature is 90, and the humidity higher. There's hardly anyone home in the morning, either, even if there were still vegetable men on their routes. Yet the demand is still there and is being met with the renaissance of the farmers' markets. Town, county, and state governments wisely support and encourage small rural farmers to get the best of their produce to the local populace.

Only a person without a soul would not revel in these affairs. Ham and sausage biscuits and fried peach and apple pies are the hearty breakfasts awaiting the daybreaking souls who know to arrive punctually. The flowers alone are worth the rise. Gladioli—pedestrian blooms in a florist's shop—shout the joy of creation. And the vegetables—potatoes still smell of the earth from which they were dug, tomatoes assert their independence from plastic packaging with every irregular shape. And for the true shopper, the ultimate satisfaction, a glib "you should have been here earlier for the baby okra" to a late-arriving neighbor.

Whatever the source, the variety of fresh vegetables on the southern table is staggering. Any one meal may present fried okra, corn, butter beans, sweet potatoes, sliced tomatoes, cucumbers and onions, coleslaw, cantaloupe. Such wealth often eclipses any meat served; by midsummer all-vegetable meals (with biscuits or corn bread) are common. By the time the pickled beets, green tomato relish, pepper relishes, bread-and-butter pickles are out, the meal is a celebration of endless kinds of combinations, textures, and flavors—the hallmark of southern cooking.

❧ Two Vegetable Puddings ❧

Here are two vegetables subjected to the same technique, and how differently we respond to each! The cabbage pudding is absolutely transcendent: we are carried from wherever and whenever that delicious aroma first reaches us—crisping pork, melting cabbage, toasting bread—to the Blue Ridge, Indian summer, some time ago. This pudding beckons us and warns us at the same time: eat heartily now, winter's over that next hill. The corn pudding seems almost frivolous in comparison, but nonetheless delicious. This food almost dances, so generously does it celebrate summer's harvest. One is lulled into thinking that sweet corn must have been out there forever, and that we will never lose it again.

Heady stuff, both these dishes—if they don't already conjure up memories for you, they will soon. Both are obviously strong enough to feature in a meal, especially for lunches. You may want a homemade tomato sauce to dress them up a little. Butter your baking dishes well, and generously sprinkle in bread crumbs. Both puddings will then invert nicely for slicing at the table.

❧ Green Corn Pudding ❧

Yields 4 servings

8 ears fresh white corn or enough
    to yield 3½ cups (875 ml) cut
    corn
3 eggs
1 cup (235 ml) milk
½ cup (118 ml) half-and-half
1 teaspoon salt
¼ teaspoon white pepper

¼ teaspoon freshly grated
    nutmeg
1 tablespoon finely chopped
    fresh basil or parsley
2 tablespoons (30 g) butter
¼ cup (60 ml) finely chopped
    scallions

Optional: ¼ cup (60 ml) finely chopped green bell pepper; 1 green cayenne pod, seeded and finely chopped

2 tablespoons cornmeal
Boiling water for the bain-marie

Recommended equipment: A medium and a large mixing bowl, 8-inch (20 cm) cast-iron skillet or enameled cast-iron sauté pan, glass or ceramic soufflé dish, and one shallow baking pan large enough to hold the soufflé dish as for a bain-marie.

Shuck and silk the corn, removing any damaged portions. Wash in cold water and drain. With a sharp knife cut down the center of each row of kernels, holding the knife blade parallel to the cob. Turn the blade horizontally and shave the kernels into a large mixing bowl. In a separate bowl, beat the 3 eggs, adding the milk and half-and-half slowly. Beat in the salt, pepper, nutmeg, and basil or parsley, and add the mixture to the corn kernels.

Melt 1 tablespoon of the butter in the skillet or sauté pan. Add the scallions and sauté very gently, taking care only to wilt them. If you decide to use the bell pepper, add it to the pan with the scallions. The cayenne, if used, should be added at the very end of the sauté. Add the sautéed vegetables to the corn and eggs, stirring to mix thoroughly.

Preheat the oven to 325°F (163°C).

Prepare the soufflé dish by coating the inside with the remaining butter. Dust the interior with the cornmeal. Pour the corn mixture into the dish and cover it with aluminum foil. Set the dish in the larger pan and add about 1 inch (2½ cm) of boiling water. Place in the middle level of the preheated oven and bake for 1½ hours, or until gently set. Add boiling water to the pan as necessary to maintain level around the soufflé dish. Water should bubble ever so slightly, but not boil. Serve from the dish or invert, turn out onto platter, and cut into wedges.

∽ Cabbage Pudding ∾

Yields 4 to 6 servings

2½ quarts (2½ L) water
2 ounces (60 g) pork sidemeat
1 dried red pepper pod
1 head of cabbage weighing
　2½ pounds (1125 g)
3 eggs
1 teaspoon salt
¼ teaspoon white pepper
⅛ teaspoon ground cayenne
¼ teaspoon ground mustard

1½ cups (355 ml) milk or half-
　and-half
¾ cup (180 ml) small cubes of
　bread from stale biscuits or
　good quality white bread
⅜ teaspoon dried thyme leaves
1 tablespoon (15 g) butter
¼ cup (60 ml) fine white bread
　crumbs
2 tablespoons (30 g) melted
　butter

Recommended equipment: An 8-quart (8 L) stockpot; small, medium, and large mixing bowls; ceramic soufflé dish.

Combine the water, sidemeat, and pepper pod in the stockpot and bring to a boil. Meanwhile trim any dark green or damaged outer leaves from the cabbage head and quarter it. Boil for 15 minutes, then refresh under cold water and drain, discarding the pepper pod and reserving the pork sidemeat. Remove the core and stem portions of the cabbage and chop roughly. Squeeze firmly between your palms or in a linen towel to remove excess moisture. Reserve in the large bowl.

In the medium bowl beat the eggs with the salt, white and cayenne peppers, and mustard. Slowly beat in the milk and add to the cabbage.

Dice the reserved pork sidemeat. Combine in the small bowl with the very small bread cubes and thyme.

Preheat the oven to 350°F (177°C).

Butter the sides and bottom of the soufflé dish and sprinkle the bread crumbs evenly over the interior of the dish. Pour in the cabbage mixture, even it out, and top with the pork sidemeat that was tossed with the bread crumbs and thyme. Drizzle the 2 tablespoons of melted butter over the surface. Bake in middle level of oven for 50 minutes or until custard is set. Invert and turn out onto a platter to slice for serving.

ᐞ Fried Vegetables ᐞ

Warm lands seem to celebrate their gift of vegetables in loving ways. I think of the *frito misto* of Italy, the savory *tians* and *gratins* of Provence. In our South, garden-fresh vegetables can take a quick dip in cornmeal and a fast turn in a skillet to bring more of a summer day to a plate than many more pretentious preparations.

For a summer lunch during the garden's zenith, serve crowder peas with vegetable relishes, fried vegetables such as cymlings and okra, sliced fresh red tomatoes, raw scallions, and corn bread—what a wonderful variety of textures, flavors, and, of course, nutrients—such a simple meal perfectly adapted to the rigors of hot weather digestion.

Those who have experienced only the travesties of southern cooking served in many restaurants may think they have reason to disagree, but vegetables fried with a respect for basic frying principles have a subtlety and delicacy that is particularly southern. Use a minimal amount of oil (preferably a natural oil such as peanut, which has no residual flavor or by-product of distillation), never crowd your pan, and keep the heat high enough to seal in the freshness. You are not stewing in oil. Regular, evenly cut pieces of vegetable are important, too; all should cook at the same rate. What vegetables to fry? Well, a southerner will fry anything, but here's a starting lineup:

All squashes (except winter)—crook neck, zucchini, cymling, or pattypan

Okra, ⅜ inch slices

Green tomatoes, thick (½ inch) slices

Onions (½ inch slices as well)—but please try to get onions as fresh from the garden as possible

Eggplant, ½ inch slices

Sweet potatoes, ⅜ inch slices

Below is a cooking guide, adapted for the native cymling, or petticoat, squash (the odd name cymling, first appearing in print in 1705, is a corruption of simnel—from the English currant cake of Lent whose flat, round shape the squash mimics). Use common sense for cooking times, and so forth, of other vegetables; for example, okra will require more fat due to its increased surface area.

❧ Fried Cymlings ❧

Yields 4 servings

4 small cymlings, petticoat, or pattypan squash approximately 6 ounces or 170 g each	9 tablespoons cornmeal
	Freshly ground black pepper
	1 teaspoon salt
3–6 tablespoons (45 g) bacon fat, peanut oil, or shortening	

Recommended equipment: A 12-inch (30 cm) cast-iron skillet or enameled cast-iron sauté pan, colander, brown paper bag.

Trim the stem and blossom ends of each cymling and cut in half vertically. Placing the cut surface down, cut each half into 6 very even wedges approximately ⅜ inch (1 cm) thick at the outer, thicker point. Rinse under running cold water in a colander and let drain.

Heat the oil, bacon fat, or shortening in the skillet or sauté pan over medium high heat. Combine the cornmeal, pepper, and salt and toss the wet slices in it, coating well all over. Carefully place the slices in the skillet so that they are not touching. Fry until golden brown— about 3 minutes—and turn carefully. Brown on the reverse side, then reserve on brown paper bag in a 250°F (121°C) oven while frying the remainder. Serve as soon as possible.

∿ Baked Tomatoes ∿

This recipe calls for the good, old-fashioned tomatoes of high-acid content. The low-acid varieties such as German Johnson won't do. Southerners like both sweet and sour flavors to complement their roasts and fried meats, and this distinctive southern penchant reflects the nineteenth-century quandary over tomatoes: Are they vegetable or fruit? In southern cooking—in salads, sauces, jellies, and pies— tomatoes remain both savory and sweet.

Yields 6 servings

6 medium tomatoes, blanched and peeled (see page xiv)	2 tablespoons brown sugar
Salt	2 cups (470 ml) stale bread cubes, about ¾ inch square
Black pepper	3 tablespoons melted butter

Recommended equipment: A 2-quart (2 L) ceramic baking dish.

Preheat oven to 350°F (177°C).

Cut the tomatoes in half and put 6 halves in the bottom of the baking dish. Sprinkle with salt, pepper, and half of the brown sugar. Pour 1 cup of the bread cubes over and drizzle with half of the melted butter. Repeat with remaining ingredients and bake at 350°F (177°C) for about 30 minutes.

∿ Mixed Beans in Egg Sauce ∿

The range of this recipe will be set by the cook—I will give you some direction, but the rest is up to you. First, use only very fresh, tender beans, and I suggest only two varieties at a time. Otherwise subtleties of contrast may be lost. My favorite combination is fresh limas and very tender flat pole beans. Snaps of all sorts, favas, butter beans, and October beans are only a few other suggestions. The secret of doing the recipe well lies in incorporating the eggs properly—the yolks must remain liquid enough to coat the beans without becoming scrambled, and the beans should not be broken in the process.

Vegetables

Yields 4 servings

2½ cups (590 ml) boiling salted water

1 garlic clove

1 pound (450 g) beans in the shell (1 cup [235 ml] or ½ pound [225 g] shelled)

½ pound (225 g) tender pole beans cut into ¾ inch (2 cm) lengths

¼ cup (60 g) butter

1 cup (235 ml) chopped onion

2 soft-boiled eggs

Salt and freshly ground black pepper

1 tablespoon freshly chopped parsley

An egg taken from the refrigerator should be boiled no more than 5 minutes. Reduce time accordingly for eggs which are at room temperature.

Recommended equipment: A 3-quart (3 L) saucepan, 12-inch (30 cm) cast-iron skillet or enameled cast-iron sauté pan with a lid.

Bring salted water to a boil in the saucepan and add unpeeled garlic clove. Shell the beans if necessary. Blanch beans separately until tender (about 12 minutes). Drain and reserve. Melt the butter over low heat in the skillet or sauté pan, add the chopped onion, and cover the pan (use aluminum foil if you don't have a lid). Sweat the onion over very low heat for 10 minutes. Do not allow the onion to color. Add the drained beans, cover, and cook for 12 more minutes, shaking the pan occasionally. Season with salt and pepper.

While beans are cooking, boil the eggs, remove them from their shells, chop them coarsely and set them aside in a dish. When ready to serve the beans, stir the eggs in quickly, turning the beans to coat them with the yolk. Add parsley and rush the beans to the table.

 *Braised Greens*

Each night the hunchback came down the stairs with the air of one who has a grand opinion of himself. He always smelled slightly of turnip greens, as Miss Amelia rubbed him night and morning with pot liquor to give him strength.

Carson McCullers, *The Ballad of the Sad Café*

John Smith remarked, "Many hearbes in the spring time there are commonly dispersed throughout the woods, good for brothes and sallets, as Violets, Purslin, Sorrell, etc. Besides many we used whose names we know not." Undoubtedly the native Americans had names for the wild greens that eventually were adopted for a southerner's mess of greens. Poke, narrow-leaved dock, creasie greens, lamb's quarter, dandelion, chickweed, chicory, and pigweed could be gathered practically throughout the year.

Of the cultivated greens, collards are probably the most nutritious, though turnip greens are the most popular throughout the region. Kale and mustard greens have their own advocates; preference varies by region. Tender greens such as spinach are not subjected to the lengthy cooking required by the coarser ones, but the seasonings for all are common: pork fat and red pepper. The well-seasoned broth is known as potlikker; it may be served with the greens, reserved for another meal and poured over corn bread, or served by itself (as every cuisine has its panaceas, southern wisdom strongly recommends potlikker for bladder ailments and hangovers). At the table condiments or garnishes are often offered. Pepper Sauce (see page 147) is added to individual taste. Crisp bacon bits, chopped hard-boiled eggs, green onions, or fresh green cayenne elevate a simple pot of greens into a more complex realm. From the Indian cuisine, the early settlers appropriated a cornmeal dumpling; dropped into the bubbling broth, it makes a nutritious, one-pot meal (see page 26).

The following recipe is a basic one for all the commonly used southern greens. Cooking time will vary according to the type of green, its maturity, and the time of year. During hot weather, it may be wise to blanch turnip or mustard greens before a final cooking to relieve them of excess bitterness. The pot should simmer, not boil. You are not overcooking a vegetable here, but braising it much in a French manner to slowly coax and develop flavors. It will be instructive for you to taste the mess of greens often, anticipating and savoring the developments.

7 cups (1¾ L) water	½ cup (118 ml) chopped onion
1½ teaspoons salt	4 tablespoons (60 g) bacon fat
⅛ to ¼ teaspoon dried red	1 teaspoon sugar
pepper flakes	2½ pounds (1125 g) greens—
2 ounces (60 g) pork sidemeat,	turnip, mustard, kale, or
diced (or a small ham hock)	collards, or a combination

Garnishes: crisp bacon bits, hard-boiled eggs, sliced green onions, chopped fresh cayenne, Pepper Sauce (see page 147), and Indian Dumplings (see page 26).

Recommended equipment: An 8-quart (8 L) stainless steel or heavy aluminum stockpot with lid.

Bring the water and seasonings to boil over high heat and boil for 20 minutes. During this time wash the greens well—usually at least twice to remove the grit. If the stems and ribs are anything but very small and tender, strip the leaf off and discard the ribs and stems. Chop large greens roughly, cook small leaves whole.

Add the greens to the pot, cover tightly, and bring back to the boil. Uncover, stir down the leaves, and reduce heat to a simmer. Cook about 1 hour. Remove greens from pot, reserving potlikker if required for future use, and serve with any of the garnishes suggested above.

∾ *Sweet Potatoes* ∾

Two different edible tubers, the sweet potato and yam, are widely raised and consumed in the South, their outward similarity leading to a confusion in names. The sweet potato is a native of the Western Hemisphere, scientifically known as *Ipomoea batatus.* Its relatives include the morning glory; native Americans consumed its taproot, occasionally finding thirty-pound specimens. The yam family is particularly widespread in the tropics; many species are still consumed in the very southern states, even more in the Caribbean. The prized species, *Discorea alata,* was brought from Africa. The etymology of yam is, in fact, a mirror of the slave trade: it comes from the Portuguese *inhame,* derived from the Senegalese *nyami*—to eat. The sweet potato is by far the more common of the two. Water content and nutritional value differ, but in cooking and in speech the two are practically interchangeable.

Below you will find two entirely different treatments of this one vegetable—a pone and a soufflé—two treatments that emphasize the disparity found in southern society of the antebellum period. The pone is so basic, so hearty that we are not surprised at the Algonquin meaning of the term pone itself: a fried bread, probably originally from the past participle meaning "baked." This pone, like a corn pone, can last several days, and often was eaten cold for breakfast. These were staple foods for settlers and natives. The black walnuts add another indigenous ingredient, one of many nuts still collected in southern forests.

Though technically not a classic soufflé and not as light as other members of that family, the Sweet Potato and Pear Soufflé is nevertheless European. This is a dish of a great planter's table, definitely an appropriate coupling with the major roasts of the winter holidays: wild boar, turkey, and venison. To me, it is a better accompaniment to game than the classic French chestnut purées. Tastes change through time, and some people may find such sweet dishes too foreign in the course of a meal; many cooks, especially those from outside the South, may want to serve both these dishes with whipped cream at the end of a meal. Add the sweetening agents cautiously and taste well. Stop when your experienced taste buds direct you to. Both these recipes are true classics, and don't neglect them because they, at first, don't seem suitable to modern tastes. Be adaptable and share your table with history.

❧ Grated Sweet Potato Pone ❧

This rich sweet potato pone should be served with simply prepared meats such as grilled chops or fried chicken. It is not appropriate for delicate seafoods or subtle sauces.

Yields 6 servings

¼ cup (60 g) butter, softened
¾ cup (151 g) light brown sugar
2 eggs
Grated zest and juice of one
   orange
Grated zest of one lemon
½ teaspoon ginger
¼ teaspoon cinnamon
¼ teaspoon white pepper
¾ teaspoon salt

2¹/₂ pounds (1125 g) sweet
  potatoes
3 tablespoons (45 g) butter

Optional: ¹/₃ cup (80 ml) finely chopped black walnuts

Recommended equipment: A blending fork or electric mixer; Mouli hand grater, stainless steel box grater, food processor, or mixer with grating attachment; 10-inch (25 cm) cast-iron skillet.

Using a blending fork or mixer, cream the ¹/₄ cup softened butter with the brown sugar until light and fluffy. Beat in the eggs and then add the fruit zest, juice of the orange, ginger, cinnamon, white pepper, and salt. Mix thoroughly and reserve.

Peel the sweet potatoes and grate them coarsely. You should have 4 to 5 cups (1 to 1¹/₄ L) tightly packed. Stir well into the egg and butter mixture and add optional black walnuts if desired.

Preheat oven to 375°F (190°C).

Melt the 3 tablespoons of butter in the skillet or baking dish over medium heat until it colors slightly. Pour the potato mixture in and spread evenly up to the edges of the pan. Increase heat to high, and cook until the first steam escapes from the cake. Immediately set on middle rack of preheated oven and bake for 40 minutes. Serve cut into wedges, hot or at room temperature.

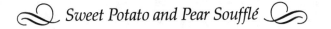 *Sweet Potato and Pear Soufflé*

This elegant preparation is particularly good with almost all game, distinctive fowl, and pork.

Yields 4 to 6 servings

3 sweet potatoes, approximate
  total weight of 1¹/₂ pounds
  (675 g)
1 tablespoon (15 g) butter
2 tablespoons dry white bread
  crumbs

3 medium, ripe pears weighing
  approximately 1 pound (450 g)
Juice of 1 lemon
¹/₈ teaspoon white pepper
¹/₂ teaspoon salt
2 tablespoons honey
2 eggs, separated

Recommended equipment: A 2-quart (2 L) glass or ceramic soufflé dish, rubber spatula.

Preheat oven to 375°F (190°C).

Poke potatoes all over with a fork and bake on an open rack in the middle level of the oven for 50 minutes, or until fully done. Remove, cut in half, and let cool. While the potatoes are cooking prepare the soufflé dish by greasing it thoroughly with the butter and thoroughly and evenly coating the interior with the bread crumbs.

Raise oven temperature to 425°F (218°C).

Peel, quarter, and core the pears, chop them coarsely and sprinkle them with the lemon juice. Reserve in a stainless steel or glass bowl. Scoop the flesh of the potatoes from their jackets with a spoon and add to the pears. Season with the pepper, salt, and honey. Beat well together, but leave mixture lumpy. Beat in egg yolks.

In a separate bowl beat the egg whites to soft peaks. Stir thoroughly one-third of the beaten whites into the potato-pear base. Very carefully fold in the remaining two-thirds of the whites. Pour into the buttered soufflé dish and bake for about 35 minutes. The center should remain slightly soft. Serve without delay.

❧ Field Peas ❧

The most important African dietary contribution to the American South is undoubtedly the *Vigna unguiculata*. It produces a rather wild-looking pod, sometimes more than a foot in length, ranging from white to pale green to deepest purple, and when ripe yields the black-eyed pea and its many cousins: crowder, field, cow, lady. By the early eighteenth century, these peas (actually more bean than pea) had reached Charleston, having already been well established in Caribbean cooking.

Like most staple dishes around the world, these legumes provide a stable background for the meal. Relief from boredom is provided by a constantly changing array of condiments: freshly chopped scallions, fresh cayenne, and pepper, pickle, and green tomato relishes. This use of condiments is one of the hallmarks of the food of the South; it is one technique for providing variety and awakening dulled palates.

Cooking time for these peas will vary greatly depending on size, variety, and freshness. Always keep enough water in the pot so the peas will remain whole. No pea is ever cooked to mushiness, though often leftover peas, especially black-eyed peas, are mashed, formed into small cakes, and fried in bacon fat.

3 pounds (1350 g) cowpeas, lady peas, crowder, or black-eyed peas (3 cups [750 ml] or 1½ pounds [675 g] shelled)
3 ounces (85 g) pork sidemeat
½ teaspoon salt

⅔ cup (160 ml) thinly sliced onions
1 bay leaf
1 red pepper pod
1 garlic clove, peeled and chopped
2½ cups (590 ml) water

Garnishes: freshly chopped green onions, green cayenne, pepper and pickle relishes, Green Tomato Relish (see page 148).

Recommended equipment: A 3-quart (3 L) saucepan.

Wash the shelled peas well and drain in a colander. Cut the sidemeat into nine strips and, along with the salt, onions, bay leaf, pepper, and garlic, simmer in the water for 15 minutes. Add the peas (and water to cover if necessary). Simmer for 35 minutes to 1 hour or longer, depending upon the maturity of the peas.

See above for garnishes to be served at the table.

 *Dried Beans*

Dried beans are an important winter staple in the southern diet. Pintos and black-eyed peas are the most frequently encountered, but white beans, October beans, "shelly" beans, and many others are also used. Simple cooking is the rule: a piece of pork fat, a pepper pod, and lots of water. Cooked dried beans usually get some kind of contrasting garnish at the table—a spoonful of chow-chow or freshly chopped onion. To almost all southerners, black or white, rich or poor, a bowl of hot pintos, cornbread, and a glass of cold buttermilk is a simple but complete meal.

Yields 5 cups cooked beans

3 to 4 ounces (90 to 120 g) pork sidemeat
1 red pepper pod

6 cups (1.5 L) water
2 cups (475 ml) dried beans
1 teaspoon salt

Recommended equipment: A 3-quart (3 L) saucepan.

Cut the sidemeat into 4 or 5 pieces and put in a saucepan with the other ingredients. Bring to a boil and simmer until beans are tender and any taste of raw starch is dissipated. Cooking time will vary from 1 to 2 or more hours depending upon the kind of bean.

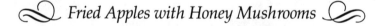 Fried Bean Cakes

Secondary meals such as Sunday night suppers and light lunches are often meatless, though never vegetarian. Southerners treasure pork fat for its flavor and its ability to fry up a crisp crust. These bean cakes have counterparts throughout African cooking; they become distinctly southern, however, when the beans are simmered with sidemeat and the cakes fried in lard. Sometimes the cakes are seasoned like pork sausage with sage and red pepper flakes, cooked for breakfast, and called "pea sausage."

Yields 4 small cakes

1 cup (235 ml) cooked, drained
    black-eyed peas (see pages
    66–67)
1 tablespoon chopped scallions

½ to 1 teaspoon chopped hot
    pepper
½ teaspoon ground cumin
Lard or bacon fat for frying

Recommended equipment: A potato masher, 8-inch (20 cm) cast-iron skillet.

Mash the beans roughly and beat in the scallions, pepper, and cumin. Shape into 4 small patties about ⅔ inch (1.7 cm) thick. Heat ¼ inch (⅝ cm) fat in the skillet. When hot but not smoking, add the bean cakes. Fry until brown and crisp, about 4 minutes; turn and brown again. Serve hot with Cajun Tomato Sauce (see page 147).

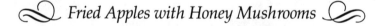 Fried Apples with Honey Mushrooms

In September, the first autumn rains bring out the wild honey mushroom *(Armillariella mellea)* briefly but abundantly. Less than one block from the busiest intersection of downtown Chapel Hill, North Carolina, lies my source, the mushrooms recurring there annually. The first picking always goes to a plump hen, which is stuffed with as many of the sautéed mushrooms as possible and roasted on a bed of fresh thyme. The bird is served with the simplest sauce—reduced pan drippings and mushrooms with the savor of fresh herbs.

The second picking soon follows, bringing with it an old mountain recipe using the first fall apples, a fit accompaniment for roasts of pork or duck. Rendered fat from the pan will serve as a sautéing medium, further binding flavors. Dried French cèpes or Italian porcini steeped in hot water or stock for ½ hour, drained, and quickly sautéed are an acceptable substitute for the honey mushroom. If you use the Champignons de Paris type of mushroom cultivated in Pennsylvania, sauté them very well to evaporate as much water as possible and concentrate their flavor.

Yields 4 servings

6 tablespoons (90 g) bacon
   grease, pan drippings, or
   butter
1½ cups (355 ml) sliced onions
4 large cooking apples, as green
   as possible

1 large garlic clove, peeled
¼ cup (50 g) sugar
1 cup (235 ml) or more honey
   mushrooms, thinly sliced

Recommended equipment: Two cast-iron skillets or enameled cast-iron sauté pans, one 10 inch (25 cm) and one 12 inch (30 cm), one with a lid.

Preheat 3 tablespoons of the fat in the skillet or sauté pan with a lid, add the onion, and sauté over low heat until tender. While the onions are cooking, peel and core the apples. Slice them thinly and add them to the onions, tossing well to distribute the onions and apples evenly. Using a garlic press, squeeze the garlic into the mixture, pour the sugar evenly over the top, shake the pan, and cover it to steam the apples. Shake the pan firmly from time to time.

Heat the remaining 3 tablespoons of fat over high heat in the other skillet or sauté pan, add the mushrooms and sauté rapidly, shaking the pan vigorously to prevent the mushrooms from burning. When the mushrooms have turned a golden brown, add them to the apples and cook off the excess moisture. Taste for seasoning (the amount of salt required will depend upon the fat being used).

Hominy is dried corn, treated chemically—traditionally and preferably with wood ash lye—to remove the husk and germ. If it is dried again and ground, it is grits, Charlestonians notwithstanding. (Confusing grits and grist, they insist hominy is the cooked milled grain, that grits are only the product of grinding.) The only ways you will get an approximation of this formerly important staple will be to start with the dried corn and treat it yourself or buy it canned. In most major northern cities with large black populations, the canned product is readily available. It is also found in Latin American markets, for hominy is integral to the widely popular Mexican stew called *pozole*. I suppose it is an acquired taste, but having acquired it so long ago, I find few foods as satisfying. Usually it is served hot and buttered, but its wonderfully neutral background seems wasted. I much prefer it "panned," as southerners say (or sautéed), with bacon, scallions, and mushrooms. Each element should retain its individual flavor and texture, playing out many variations on a stable theme.

This can be a very pretty dish as well—flecks of crispy brown bacon, green scallions, and red pimentos—good with fried chicken, ribs, or pork chops. In a land where many starchy vegetables are consumed at one meal, it seems appropriate to include hominy in this chapter for, before grinding, hominy is considered a vegetable by most southerners.

Yields 4 servings

6 slices bacon, approximately 5 ounces (140 g)

2 cups (475 ml) sliced mushrooms

¾ cup (180 ml) scallions, chopped

1 clove garlic, minced

1 20-ounce (565 g) can hominy, drained

2 tablespoons chopped pimento

½ teaspoon salt

Freshly ground black pepper

2 tablespoons chopped fresh parsley

Recommended equipment: A 12-inch (30 cm) cast-iron skillet or enameled cast-iron sauté pan.

Drain hominy in sieve and set aside.

Cut each piece of bacon lengthwise, and then cut into squares. Place in the cold skillet or sauté pan and render over low to medium heat until the bacon browns. Remove it before it becomes crisp. In crease heat and add the sliced mushrooms, sautéing well until liquid evaporates. Add the scallions and minced garlic, stirring well until the scallions wilt. Increase heat to high and add the hominy. Continue stirring and add the pimento, salt, reserved bacon, and pepper. Remove from heat, stir in the fresh parsley, and serve immediately.

❧ Okra Beignets ❧

Devotees of the *Hibiscus esculentus* will welcome this recipe, for it not only functions well as an accompaniment to a main dish, but also makes a great hot hors d'oeuvre, passed in a napkin-lined basket. American Indians and blacks from Louisiana would scoff at our belated discovery of okra's versatility; among their many traditional uses of this pod was roasting the seeds for a coffee substitute.

Yields 4 servings

2 cups (475 ml) okra, very thinly sliced	½ cup (118 ml) well-cooked rice or 5 tablespoons fine, dry bread crumbs
⅔ cup (160 ml) minced onion	1 egg
5 tablespoons minced green bell pepper	½ teaspoon Tabasco sauce
3 tablespoons flour	1 tablespoon light cream
½ teaspoon salt	6 tablespoons (90 g) shortening

Recommended equipment: A medium mixing bowl, 8-inch (20 cm) cast-iron skillet or enameled cast-iron sauté pan, slotted spoon, brown paper bag.

Toss the okra with the onion and green pepper in a mixing bowl. Sprinkle the flour and salt over all and toss again. Stir in either the rice or the bread crumbs. Beat the egg with the Tabasco sauce and the light cream. Pour over the vegetable mixture, fold in lightly, and let sit at room temperature for 20 minutes.

Heat the shortening in the skillet or sauté pan over medium high heat. Drop the okra by tablespoon into the hot fat. Fry for 2 minutes, or until golden brown, turn with a slotted spoon and finish frying. When done, remove with the slotted spoon and drain on the brown paper bag.

Fish and Shellfish

And in diverse places, that abundance of fish lying so thicke with their heads above the water, as for want of nets (our barge driving amongst them) we attempted to catch them with a frying pan; but we found it a bad instrument to catch fish with. Neither better fish, more plenty or variety, had any of us ever seene in any place, swimming in the water, then in the bay of Chesapeack: but there not to be caught with frying pans.

John Smith, *The Proceedings of the English Colony in Virginia*

The almost comical abundance of fish and shellfish described by John Smith was crucial for the survival of all European coastal settlers. The oyster alone saved some Jamestown colonists from starvation in the winter of 1609: "this want of corne occasioned the end of all our works, it being worke sufficient to provide victual. 60. or 80. with Ensigne Laxon was sent down the river to live upon Oysters." Elsewhere, Cabeza de Vaca, who was marooned on the Gulf of Mexico, lived with Indians who survived on oysters from February to April, erecting their huts over the piles of discarded shells.

Later, John Smith assayed the regular Virginia catch, a description to entice more Europeans to American shores: "Sturgeon, Grampus, Porpus, Seales, Stingraies whose tails are very dangerous. Brettes, mullets, white Salmonds, Trowts, Soles, Plaice, Herrings, Conyfish, Rockfish, Eeles, Lampreyes, Catfish, Shades, Pearch of 3 sorts, Crabs, Shrimps, Creuises, Oysters, Cocles, and Muscles."

From the Indians, the Jamestown settlers learned native techniques of procuring and preparing fish. Without iron, the Indians fashioned hooks from bone and wood. Spears and dip-nets were part of the aboriginal equipment, as well as lassoes for the taking of sturgeon. Poisons extracted from the buckeye and the devil's shoestring paralyzed fish for easy harvesting. Fish traps and weirs—upright poles in the water with lathes interwoven—worked with the currents, as did rock traps, remains of which are still discernible in inland rivers. This catch could go into various kinds of stews; the Indians would "boil Fish as well as Flesh with their Homony," reported Robert Beverly in *Virginia* in 1705.

The more important methods of open fire preparation were noted by the earliest explorers and were greatly admired in England. Another ancient technique—sun drying fish—is still practiced. On a bright day the prospect is every bit as amusing as skillet fishing; pinned to clotheslines in the backyards of eastern Virginia and North Carolina, heavily salted and peppered fat herring swing gently in the breeze.

Inland as well, the Indian and frontier diet was often dependent on aquatic life, especially during seasons that were poor hunting times. Excavations of the middens, or shell mounds, of the Tennessee River Valley revealed fifty-six species of freshwater mussels and twenty-nine species of freshwater snails used as food in a single native-inhabited site. At Moundville, Alabama, the most sophisticated Indian society in the American Southeast established fish ponds. Four lakes were located within the protective compound. Stocked with fish, these natural storage tanks provided a ready, convenient source of live food—even during siege.

As true domestication of food animals in the colonies became a reality, the dependence on fish and shellfish lessened for both the Europeans and the native Americans. But in the earliest days the permanence of the coastal settlements was established on the abundance of marine life. Many southern fish and shellfish recipes reveal this strong heritage of indigenous techniques and ingredients, and the various combinations of corn and fish are one example.

ᘓᕲ Currituck Roast Mullet ᕲᘔ

Yields 4 servings

On a cool, fall evening open bonfires flare up along the riversides and beaches from eastern Maryland to North Carolina. The heady aroma of hardwood smoke and the sharpness of the air set up appetites in anticipation of an annual fish roast. Mullets are at their fattest; impaled on green sticks, they will roast slowly before the flames. The Indians were preparing fish in this manner when the first European settlers arrived. The colonists adopted the method immediately; artists sent to record the New World natives repeatedly drew them at fish roasts. A contemporary description of today's fish roast by Mrs. Walton Griggs in the *Roanoke Island Cook Book* is an authentic descendant of the original. A fish roast "takes place when the mullet are running in the fall. Use 4 fresh mullet. Dress, leaving the heads on. Insert sharp pointed juniper sticks in the fish's mouth and hold slanting over a bed of live hardwood oak coals, turning occasionally. Within a half-hour the fish are done. Mullets are especially suitable because in the late fall they are fat and do not dry out in the cooking process. Cornbread, coleslaw, and baked sweet potatoes are served with fish."

ᘓᕲ Fried Fish ᕲᘔ

Southerners fry fish or shellfish in three very different coatings. In the inland South cornmeal coating was the original method of choice for preparing freshwater catfish, crappies, and bream and actually became the definition of fried fish.

Around Charleston and other French-influenced areas, the classic *à l'anglaise* technique was favored. The fish is dusted with flour, dipped into beaten egg, and rolled in very fine bread or cracker crumbs. Local restaurants call it "crumb-fried" or "cracker-fried" which belies the sophistication of the process.

Calabash-style is the third fish frying mode of the South. The name comes from a small fishing village on the North Carolina coast. Featured in a *Life* magazine article, the seafood restaurants of Calabash became famous nationally and proliferated, obliterating whatever charm the sleepy little town once enjoyed. In cooking, Calabash-style means a light flour batter.

1 cup (122 g) cornmeal	2 pounds (900 g) fish fillets:
½ cup (61 g) flour	bluefish, catfish, croakers,
1 teaspoon black pepper	flounder, whatever
¼ teaspoon cayenne pepper	1 cup (235 ml) buttermilk
½ teaspoon paprika	Vegetable shortening and lard
1½ to 2 teaspoons salt	

Recommended equipment: A 10-inch (25 cm) cast-iron skillet.

Mix the dry ingredients well. Pour the buttermilk over the fish and let marinate 5 to 10 minutes.

Melt enough fat in the skillet to make a layer about ¼ inch (⅝ cm) deep. Remove the fish from the buttermilk, shake off the excess liquid, and dip both sides into the cornmeal. Shake off excess coating, but gently pat what remains so it will adhere. Arrange fish in hot skillet without crowding and fry over medium high heat, about 3 minutes on each side depending on the thickness of the fillet.

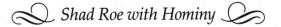 *Shad Roe with Hominy*

The shad is so bony that many folks forego the pleasures of its delicious flesh. One old and still popular southern recipe eradicates the bones and with them most of the other reasons for eating this fish in the first place. For "Shad without Bones" a large (four pounds or so) fish is cleaned and rubbed inside and out with vinegar and butter. Wrapped and sealed in foil, it is baked, covered in a casserole, for 6 to 8 hours at 250° F, or until the bones disintegrate.

One good reason this fish is pursued in the stream and marketplace is its roe. When the egg-rich females leave the Atlantic to spawn in their ancestral freshwater streams of the East Coast, they often carry more roe by weight than accessible flesh. Females will command a much higher price than their lowly paramours, called bucks; many are purchased only for the roe. The combination of fish and hominy was a favorite of native Americans, who shared it with the early settlers at Jamestown. The pork and sherry of our recipe come directly from the Europeans, and the tomato had to cross the Atlantic twice before it ended up on American tables. This wonderfully hybrid result reflects many of the roots of southern cooking.

3 tablespoons (45 g) butter, melted

1 pound (450 g) fresh shad roe, preferably 2 sets

Juice of 1 lemon

¼ cup (60 ml) water

Salt

Freshly ground black pepper

8 slices bacon (approximately 7 ounces or 190 g)

½ cup (118 ml) finely chopped onion

2 garlic cloves, finely chopped

¼ teaspoon dried thyme

3 medium, ripe tomatoes (blanched, peeled, and seeded; see page xiv), chopped to yield 1½ cups (355 ml)

2 tablespoons dry sherry

1 16-ounce (450 g) can of hominy, drained

2 tablespoons fresh, chopped parsley

Lemon wedges for garnish

Recommended equipment: A baking dish, waxed paper, two cast-iron skillets or enameled cast-iron sauté pans, one 10 inch (25 cm) and one 12 inch (30 cm).

Preheat oven to 350°F (177°C).

Pour the melted butter into the baking dish and carefully arrange the shad roe in it. Sprinkle with lemon juice and pour the water around but not over the roe. Season with salt and pepper. Cover loosely with waxed paper and bake on the middle level of the pre-heated oven until the shad roe is firm and has just set up—about 20 minutes depending upon the size of the roe. Remove and let cool. Separate the pairs of roe.

Using the larger skillet or sauté pan, cook the bacon until crisp, starting it in a cold pan. Remove and crumble the bacon when cool, reserving it as a final garnish. Pour one-half of the rendered bacon fat into the other skillet or sauté pan for sautéing the roe. Meanwhile, sauté the onions in the skillet used for the bacon. When the onion is lightly browned, stir in the garlic and the thyme and cook 1 minute. Add the tomatoes and simmer for 20 minutes, adding water if neces-sary to maintain the consistency of a sauce. Stir in the sherry and boil rapidly for 2 minutes. Add the drained hominy and heat thoroughly. Reserve and keep warm.

Heat the bacon fat in the smaller skillet or sauté pan and, handling the roe carefully, sauté it until golden brown on both sides.

Divide the tomato sauce with hominy evenly among four plates. Place the sautéed roe on top of the sauce and sprinkle with fresh parsley and the crumbled bacon. Garnish with lemon wedges and serve very hot.

❧ Corn Oyster Fritters ☙

These fritters make an excellent first course or luncheon entrée, though in the South they are usually served alongside a meat dish. In Maryland and Virginia, they accompany fried chicken.

Yields 4 servings

1 cup (235 ml) chopped, drained
   oysters
4 eggs, separated
1 cup (235 ml) fresh corn, grated
¼ cup (60 ml) minced onion
½ cup (61 g) flour

¾ teaspoon salt
6 grindings fresh pepper
⅛ teaspoon nutmeg
1 tablespoon fresh, chopped
   parsley

Fat for frying: vegetable oil or lard

Recommended equipment: A box grater, two mixing bowls, a 12-inch (30 cm) cast-iron skillet or deep fryer, frying thermometer, rubber spatula, slotted spoon, brown paper bag.

Chop and drain the oysters and reserve. Separate the eggs. Beat the yolks and add the grated or finely cut fresh corn along with the onion. Slowly add flour while stirring until evenly mixed. Add the oysters and seasonings. When ready to begin frying, heat ½ inch (1¼ cm) of fat in the skillet to 360°F (182°C). Beat the egg whites until stiff and fold into the oyster-corn mixture. Drop by spoonfuls into the fat. Cook about 90 seconds, or until golden brown, then turn carefully with the slotted spoon. When brown on the other side, remove and drain on brown paper bag. Serve as soon as possible.

❧ Crab Cakes ☙

Maryland is famous for its crab cakes, and for a birthday one year, we went on a crab-eating tour from Annapolis to Baltimore. The steamed crabs set afire by Old Bay, the traditional Maryland seasoning, were succulent, but the crab cakes were more bread than crab and too sweetly rich from commercial mayonnaise. Below are the crab cakes we serve at Crook's Corner with various sauces—tartar, brown butter and capers, mango salsa, or beurre blanc.

Yields 8 crab cakes

1 pound (454 g) picked backfin crab
1 extra large egg, beaten
¼ cup (120 ml) half-and-half
3 slices stale white bread, crusts removed and cut into very small cubes

1 tablespoon fresh, chopped parsley
1½ tablespoons fresh, chopped scallions
1 pinch freshly grated nutmeg
4 tablespoons grated Parmesan
Grated zest of ½ lemon
Salt, pepper, cayenne to taste

Combine all the ingredients and toss lightly until well mixed. Do not compact the mixture, or handle it so roughly that the crab shreds and loses its identity. Try to keep the chunks intact. Chill for about an hour, then form into 2½-ounce patties.

The crab cakes may be fried in butter as they are. They are more delicate dipped into flour, then into egg beaten with a little water, and finally coated in bread crumbs. The French call this technique *á l'anglaise*; it may be performed 30 or 40 minutes before cooking.

Mountain Trout with Bacon and Scallions

Bacon frying is almost always irresistible. In a mountain forest, by a limpid stream, at sunset, over an open fire, it beckons more seductively than Circe . When coupled with the reward of an honest fisherman—fresh trout fried till crisp, ash-roasted baby potatoes, and, in the spring, perhaps a handful of freshly chopped ramps tossed into the sputtering fat—it creates my idea of a great meal: strong, fresh flavors in equal combat, food that sustains, not just entertains. This recipe for trout is a bit of a refinement on such camp cooking, but not too much so. A light cornmeal dusting adds flavor and crispness to the fish, and the scallions will permit a quicker reentry to society than their obstreperous wild cousin, the ramp, but the essence of the dish remains the same.

With simple equipment, an indoor fireplace can become a camp fire, too. Beyond a good bed of coals, you'll need four to eight bricks to support an oven rack above the heat source. Use an unscented soap bar to coat the rack and the bottom of the skillet—afterwards any blackening washes away quickly. Roast potatoes in their jackets covered well in hot ashes, not coals.

Beyond mountain trout, you may use any flavorful ocean fish: drums, blues, channel bass, even mackerel, and they may be filleted or cut into steaks. The delicacy of a sole or flounder will be obscured by the bacon and scallions. Small, whole fish will re-create the original nature of the dish best, though, that of the fisherman's repast. Leave the heads on; their presence prevents moisture loss and provides an additional delicacy: the cheek. To placate squeamish diners, replace the eyes after cooking with a whole caper or a bit of black olive.

Yields 4 servings

4 mountain trout, cleaned but left with head intact (12 ounces or 340 g each, dressed weight)

$\frac{1}{4}$ teaspoon salt and freshly ground black pepper

$\frac{3}{4}$ cup (180 ml) yellow cornmeal

$\frac{1}{4}$ cup (60 ml) flour

1 teaspoon salt

6 tablespoons peanut oil

6 slices bacon, diced (approximately 5 ounces or 140 g)

2 cups (475 ml) sliced scallions

2 tablespoons apple cider vinegar or lemon juice

2 tablespoons freshly chopped parsley

$\frac{1}{2}$ teaspoon salt

Freshly ground black pepper

Black olives or capers (optional)

Recommended equipment: One or two 12-inch (30 cm) cast-iron skillets or enameled cast-iron sauté pans, brown paper bag.

Wash the fish well under running cold water. Dry the cavity and outside thoroughly with paper towels. Make 2 diagonal slashes $\frac{1}{4}$ inch ($\frac{2}{3}$ cm) deep and 1 inch ($2\frac{1}{2}$ cm) long on each side of the fish at the thickest point. Sprinkle the $\frac{1}{4}$ teaspoon of salt and a dash of freshly ground black pepper inside each one. Combining the cornmeal, flour, and salt, coat each fish lightly but thoroughly and reserve.

Add the peanut oil and bacon to the cold skillet or sauté pan. Heat slowly to moderate, browning the bacon. Remove the bacon and reserve. Ensuring that the pan is hot, place two trout in it and brown well on each side, about 10 to 12 minutes in all. (If you have two skillets that will accommodate two fish each, divide fat and bacon between them and cook all four at once.) If you have any doubts as to doneness,

Fish and Shellfish

check the spine at the center of the abdominal cavity: it should be opaque. Drain fish on brown paper bag and hold in a warm oven while you fry the remaining fish and prepare the sauce.

Increase heat to high. Add the scallions and stir until just wilted. Pour in vinegar or lemon juice and boil down rapidly. Stir in bacon and parsley; check for seasoning. Transfer fish to a warm serving platter, pour the bubbling sauce over all, and serve immediately.

∾ Oyster and Veal Sausage ∾

This peculiar sausage is an antique recipe from the eastern shores of the Chesapeake Bay. As a breakfast meat, it is much lower in fat than pork sausage, and so delicate it is perhaps best at lunch or light suppers.

Yields about 2 pounds

4 ounces (115 g) butter
1/2 cup (118 ml) chopped mushrooms
1/2 cup (118 ml) chopped onions
8 ounces (225 g) lean veal with no fat or tendons
2 cups (475 ml) stale, small white bread cubes
3 tablespoons chopped fresh parsley
1/8 teaspoon freshly grated nutmeg

1/8 teaspoon ground cayenne pepper
1/2 teaspoon ground white pepper
1 teaspoon salt
2 cups (475 ml) raw, shucked oysters
1 egg
Flour, salt, and freshly ground black pepper for dredging
Butter or bacon fat for frying

Optional: Hog intestine casings for making link sausages. (See page 96 for more information on using casings.)

Recommended equipment: A meat grinder, grinder attachment for electric mixer, or an excellent chopping knife; 8-inch (20 cm) cast-iron skillet or enameled cast-iron sauté pan; mixing bowl; sausage horn for grinder if making link sausage.

Melt the butter in the skillet or sauté pan and sauté the mushrooms and onions well, until all moisture is evaporated. Let cool and turn into a mixing bowl. Chop the veal coarsely if using a grinder or very finely if using a knife or cleaver. Add to the bowl along with the small stale bread cubes, parsley, nutmeg, peppers, and salt. Chop the raw, shucked oysters coarsely in the same manner as the veal. Beat the egg and add it, mixing all well. If using a grinder, run the mixture through to your desired consistency, coarse or fine. (If you plan to stuff the casings, a finer consistency will be preferable.)

At this point, form some sausage into a patty, dredge in the flour, salt, and pepper mix and fry until golden on each side. Taste for seasoning and correct if necessary. Sausage may be fried as patties, or, if made into links, poached in simmering water for 5 minutes and then gently browned in a skillet. In either case, use the mixture within 24 hours.

 Two Coastal Shellfish Pies

The most elegant versions of southern shellfish pies come from Maryland, where a puff pastry crust is filled with plump oysters and mushrooms in a cream sauce. Farther south, the dish becomes much less formal and more a casserole, with baked breads serving as a crust. The first recipe below comes from the Rappahannock River area of Virginia, where fine local oysters are especially prized. The shrimp pie is found in many variations from lower North Carolina through Florida.

Oyster Pie

Yields 4 to 6 servings

3 tablespoons (45 g) butter
2½ cups (590 ml) fresh
　mushrooms, sliced
Juice of 1 lemon
1¼ cups (295 ml) sliced scallions
2 garlic cloves, finely chopped
¼ cup (60 ml) freshly chopped
　parsley
½ teaspoon salt
¼ teaspoon ground cayenne
　pepper

¼ teaspoon freshly grated
　nutmeg
12 slices fresh white bread
3 tablespoons (45 g) melted
　butter
2½ cups (590 ml) fresh, shucked
　oysters
1 cup (235 ml) heavy cream
Freshly ground black pepper
1 cup (235 ml) fresh, coarsely
　grated bread crumbs

3 tablespoons (45 g) butter
Butter for greasing the baking
   dish

Recommended equipment: A 10-inch (25 cm) cast-iron skillet or enameled cast-iron sauté pan, baking dish, colander.

Melt the 3 tablespoons of butter in the skillet or sauté pan over medium high heat and sauté the mushrooms well, until lightly browned. Sprinkle with the lemon juice; add the scallions and garlic, cooking until just wilted. Add the seasonings: parsley, salt, cayenne, and nutmeg.

Preheat oven broiler. Trim away the crusts from the bread and brush the bread lightly with the melted butter and toast each side until golden. Grease the baking dish and turn oven heat to 425°F (218°C).

Put 6 slices of the toast in the baking dish. Drain the oysters in the colander and cover the toast evenly with them. Grind a generous amount of pepper over the shellfish. Spoon one-half of the mushroom mixture over the oysters, and pour ½ cup of the heavy cream over all. Top with 6 more slices of toast, spoon on the remaining mushrooms, and pour the remaining cream over the entire casserole. Sprinkle the top with the bread crumbs and dot with butter. Bake on the bottom level of the preheated oven for 15 to 20 minutes until the cream bubbles and the top browns. Serve as the main feature of an informal luncheon or supper. A watercress salad would be a tasty accompaniment.

❧ Shrimp and Corn Pie ❧

Yields 4 servings

2 tablespoons (30 g) melted
   butter
6 to 9 cooked biscuits (Raised
   Biscuits or Angel Biscuits, see
   pages 35 and 36)
2 tablespoons (30 g) butter
1½ cups (355 ml) sliced small
   mushrooms
½ cup (118 ml) scallions,
   chopped

½ cup (118 ml) red or green bell
   pepper, chopped
1 cup (235 ml) cut fresh corn (2
   large ears)
¼ teaspoon white pepper
¼ teaspoon ground cayenne
   pepper
⅛ teaspoon freshly grated
   nutmeg
½ teaspoon salt

1 pound (450 g) large shrimp,
   peeled and deveined
2 tablespoons dry sherry
3 eggs
1 cup (235 ml) milk

Recommended equipment: A baking dish, 10-inch (25 cm) cast-iron skillet or enameled cast-iron sauté pan.

Preheat broiler. Melt 2 tablespoons of butter over low heat. Split the biscuits and line the bottom of the baking dish with them. Brush the split halves well with melted butter and toast under the broiler until golden and crisp.

In the skillet or sauté pan, melt the additional 2 tablespoons of butter and sauté the mushrooms well over medium heat. Stir in the scallions and bell pepper and cook until just wilted. Remove from heat and pour the vegetables into a mixing bowl with the corn, white pepper, cayenne, nutmeg, and salt. Preheat oven to 325°F (163°C).

Toss the shrimp with the sherry. Beat the eggs with the milk and pour over the vegetables. Arrange the shrimp over the biscuits. Stir any liquid into the vegetable mixture and pour over the shrimp and biscuits. Bake in middle level of oven for 50 minutes, or until custard is set. Do not brown or let puff.

ᜥ Crayfish Etouffé ᜥ

"Etouffé" means smothered, but you won't find these crayfish under a pillow; instead they're awash in a rich buttery Cajun sauce, this time without tomatoes. Shrimp may be substituted if your fish market doesn't sell live crayfish. I can't recommend frozen crayfish, but with the spread of crayfish farms up the East Coast, special orders of live crayfish should be feasible for almost any part of the country. Crayfish are not easy to peel, and they will take some time. If you're a novice, it might be wise to prepare the crayfish a day in advance. One advantage of a large family will surely cross your mind. Are crayfish really worth the effort? If you truly appreciate subtlety and delicacy in taste, the answer is yes.

Yields 4 to 6 servings

The crayfish

7 to 8 pounds (3.175 to 3.6 kg)
   live crayfish
Shrimp, Crab, or Crayfish Boil
   (see page 85)

The stock

4 cups (1 L) cooked crayfish
   shells and heads, 2½ cups (590
   ml) water, ½ cup (118 ml) dry
   white wine; OR
3 cups (705 ml) fresh seafood
   stock; OR

2 cups (475 ml) clam juice and 1
   cup (235 ml) water
1 cup (235 ml) chopped onion
½ cup (118 ml) chopped celery
1 bay leaf
1 teaspoon thyme
20 black peppercorns

The roux

4 tablespoons (60 g) lard, bacon
   fat, or shortening
4 tablespoons flour

Aromatic vegetables

¾ cup (180 ml) chopped onion
½ cup (118 ml) chopped celery
½ cup (118 ml) chopped red or
   green bell pepper
2 garlic cloves, chopped

Final seasonings and enrichment

2 teaspoons salt
1 teaspoon ground cayenne
¾ teaspoon ground white pepper
1 teaspoon thyme

½ teaspoon dried basil
1½ cups (355 ml) sliced scallions
¼ pound (115 g) butter

Serve with 3 cups (705 ml) hot, cooked rice

Recommended equipment: A 4-quart (4 L) saucepan, 12-inch (30 cm) cast-iron skillet or enameled cast-iron sauté pan.

Preparation of crayfish
For live crayfish see page 86 for Shrimp, Crab, or Crayfish Boil recipe, cooking 3 to 5 minutes, depending on size. Allow about 1¹/₂ hours for peeling this much crayfish the first time. Reserve 4 cups (1 L) of shells and heads for stock.

Stock
In the saucepan, combine crayfish shells, water, and wine with the onion, celery, bay, thyme, and peppercorns. Simmer 20 minutes and strain carefully. If you are using previously prepared stock or clam juice, fortify it by simmering with the above flavoring ingredients as well.

Roux
In the skillet or sauté pan heat the fat until it melts. Whisk in the flour and cook slowly over medium heat, watching it carefully and stirring often, until it turns a deep, dark brown, roughly the color of dark brown sugar. This should take about 25 to 30 minutes—the color must change *very* slowly or the result will be a bitter-tasting roux.

Immediately stir in the chopped aromatic vegetables, remove from heat, and let sit for 5 minutes, stirring frequently to dissipate the heat of the pan. Stir in the strained stock and return to heat, simmering for 30 minutes.

Add cooked, shelled, crayfish tails and final seasonings of salt, cayenne, white pepper, thyme, basil, and scallions. Bring to a low boil and whisk in the butter, a tablespoon at a time. Serve immediately with freshly cooked rice.

♫ Shrimp, Crab, or Crayfish Boil ♫

Through there came a smell of garlic and cloves and red pepper, a blast of hot cloud escaped from a cauldron they could see now on a stove at the back of the other room. A massive back, presumably female, with a twist of gray hair on top, stood with a ladle akimbo. A young man joined her and with his fingers stole something out of the pot and ate it. At Baba's they were boiling shrimp.

Eudora Welty, "No Place for You, My Love"

Yields about 1 cup or enough for 10 to 12 pounds of shellfish

2 teaspoons whole celery seed
8 teaspoons whole mustard seed
8 teaspoons whole black
  peppercorns

12 bay leaves, crumbled
12 dried red pepper pods,
  quartered
24 whole cloves

Combine above ingredients, mix well, bottle, and store.

To boil seafood

3 pounds (1350 g) shrimp, crab,
  or crayfish in the shell
4 quarts (4 L) water
5 tablespoons Shrimp, Crab, or
  Crayfish Boil (see above)

4 teaspoons salt
1 onion, sliced
2 whole garlic cloves

Recommended equipment: An 8- to 16-quart (8 to 15 L) stockpot.

Combine all ingredients except seafood in stockpot and bring to a boil over high heat. Reduce heat and cook for 20 minutes.

During this time, using shrimp as the example, wash them under running cold water and drain in a colander. At the end of the 20-minute period, add the shrimp and cook for 3 minutes. Check the largest shrimp—if done it will be opaque throughout. If more cooking is required, turn off heat and let sit, checking frequently. Unless shrimp are grotesquely sized, they should be done in less than 5 minutes.

Crayfish will cook in the same time as shrimp of equal size. Hard-shelled blue crabs will need about 12 to 15 minutes of cooking.

 *Low Country Shrimp Pâté*

A seafood pâté makes an elegant first course with an herb mayonnaise or green sauce. The traditional Carolina version, however, is served on toast, more often with drink than at the table.

Yields 6 to 8 servings

1 tablespoon (15 g) butter
4 ounces (115 g) lightly smoked
  ham, very thinly sliced
1½ pounds (675 g) raw shrimp,
  peeled

2 egg whites
1 whole egg
1 tablespoon sherry
1 tablespoon lemon juice
4 ounces (115 g) butter, softened

1¼ teaspoons salt

½ teaspoon white pepper

¼ teaspoon freshly grated
   nutmeg

⅛ teaspoon ground cayenne

Zest of one lemon, finely grated

2 tablespoons chopped, fresh
   parsley

¼ cup (60 ml) heavy cream

Boiling water for a bain-marie

Recommended equipment: A loaf pan and a larger pan to form a bain-marie, blender or food processor, box grater, aluminum foil.

Preheat oven to 400°F (204°C).

Grease the loaf pan with the tablespoon of butter and line the bottom and sides with the ham. There should be enough ham left to top the finished pâté.

Divide the shrimp into three equal portions in three bowls. Put an egg white in each of the first two bowls and the whole egg in the third. Purée each portion separately. To the first, add 1 tablespoon of sherry while blending. To the second, add 1 tablespoon of lemon juice. To the third, add the 4 ounces of softened butter. Combine the three batches of puréed shrimp in a mixing bowl and beat well with the salt, white pepper, nutmeg, cayenne, lemon zest, and chopped parsley. Beat the ¼ cup heavy cream until soft peaks form. Fold into the shrimp mixture and spoon all into the lined pan. Smooth out the mixture and top with the reserved ham; cover tightly with aluminum foil. Place the loaf pan into the larger pan and add 1 inch (2½ cm) of boiling water to form a bain-marie. Bake for approximately 35 minutes, or until pâté is firm in the center and the sides have pulled away slightly from the pan. Cool the pâté in its pan on a rack and turn out when cool. Refrigerate at least three hours before serving; slice very thinly—about ⅛ inch (⅓ cm).

∽ *Deep Fried Shrimp with Brown Onions and Grits* ∾

Shrimp and grits are a popular combination from Wilmington, North Carolina, to the northern Florida coast. Carolinians attribute remarkable properties of increasing longevity to eating it regularly for breakfast. Often the shrimp are sautéed in bacon fat and served with a gravy spiked with onion and green pepper over grits. Below is a more sophisticated and complicated version in which the grits are a remarkably effective foil for bringing out all the flavor of the crispy and quickly cooked fried shrimp and the contrasting slowly braised caramelized onions. This is a stunning seafood dish served among many courses of a formal dinner.

Yields 4 to 6 servings

2 tablespoons (30 g) bacon fat
2 tablespoons (30 g) butter
7 cups (1650 ml) very thinly
    sliced onions
1/4 cup (60 ml) water
1/2 teaspoon salt
1/2 teaspoon freshly ground black
    pepper
Juice of 1 lemon
8 tablespoons flour
10 tablespoons cold water

1 teaspoon salt
2 tablespoons chopped, fresh
    parsley
2 tablespoons chopped scallions
2 egg whites
1 1/4 pounds (565 g) large, raw
    shrimp, peeled
Peanut oil sufficient to cover a
    skillet to the depth of 1/4 inch
    (2/3 cm)
3 cups (705 ml) hot, cooked grits

Recommended equipment: Two cast-iron skillets or enameled cast-iron sauté pans with covers, preferably a 10-inch pan (25 cm) for the onions and a 12-inch pan (30 cm) for frying the shrimp; electric mixer; rubber spatula; frying thermometer; slotted spoon; brown paper bag.

Melt the bacon fat and butter in a skillet or sauté pan over medium high heat. Add the sliced onions and cook until just tender. Add water, salt, and pepper, cover and cook over medium heat for 30 minutes. Remove cover and cook off liquid. Continue cooking slowly until onions reach a deep shade of brown. It is very important to prevent even the slightest burning or scorching. Reduce heat or add a small amount of water to slow down the cooking if necessary. Season with lemon juice when done and ready to serve.

For the shrimp batter combine flour, cold water, salt, parsley, and scallions, and stir until smooth. Let rest for 30 minutes before using. When ready to fry the shrimp, beat the egg whites stiffly and fold into the batter with the rubber spatula.

Preheat the oil in the other skillet to 365°F (185°C). Battering the shrimp a few at a time, add them to the skillet, fry gently on each side, and drain on brown paper bag.

Place hot, buttered grits on individual plates. Divide the onions evenly and top with the hot batter-fried shrimp. Serve immediately.

Shrimp and Grits, Crook's Corner Style

Shrimp and Grits is undoubtedly the most requested recipe I have yet created. In 1985 Craig Claiborne visited Crook's Corner in Chapel Hill for dinner and sampled many dishes. After dinner he asked me to prepare Shrimp and Grits for him in my kitchen the next morning. Mr. Claiborne, who is a champion of southern foods, especially grits, later published this and several other recipes from my book in the *New York Times,* and the craze was on. Now we serve over 10,000 plates of Shrimp and Grits a year at Crook's Corner. Here is the "real" recipe.

Yields 4 servings

1 recipe Basic Boiled Grits (see page 30)
Tabasco sauce
Freshly grated nutmeg
White pepper
1 pound (454 g) fresh shrimp
6 slices bacon
Peanut oil
2 cups (470 ml) sliced mushrooms

1 cup (235 ml) finely sliced scallions
1 large garlic clove, peeled
4 teaspoons lemon juice
Tabasco sauce
2 tablespoons fresh, chopped parsley
Salt and pepper

Recommended equipment: A 10-inch (25 cm) skillet, garlic press.

Prepare the grits according to the recipe using the full amount of cheese. Season to taste, but lightly, with Tabasco, a very little nutmeg, and white pepper. Hold in a warm place or in the top of a double boiler over simmering water.

Peel the shrimp, rinse, and pat dry.

Dice the bacon and sauté lightly in the skillet. The edges of the bacon should brown, but the bacon should not become crisp.

Add enough peanut oil to the bacon fat in the skillet to make a layer of fat about 1/8-inch (.35 cm) deep. When quite hot, add the shrimp in an even layer. Turn the shrimp as they start to color, add the mushrooms, and sauté about 4 minutes. Turn occasionally and add the scallions. Add the garlic through the press and stir around. Then season with lemon juice, a dash or two of Tabasco, and parsley. Add salt and pepper to taste.

Divide the grits among four plates. Spoon the shrimp over and serve immediately.

Chicken, veal, pork chops, seafood—any meat may be made Creole by simmering in the sauce of this recipe. Shrimp is the classic and the best-known rendition, but it is basic Creole cooking. Leftovers are tossed with boiled rice and come out jambalayas. Extended with liquid and thickened with a roux and okra, a Creole sauce is gumbo. There is no better way to start in on Creole cooking than with this straightforward recipe.

Yields 6 to 8 servings

2 pounds (900 g) shrimp
1/4 cup (60 ml) bacon fat
1 1/2 cups (350 ml) chopped onion
3 cups (700 ml) chopped sweet
   red and green pepper
1 cup (235 ml) chopped celery
1 to 2 teaspoons fresh, chopped
   cayenne pepper, seeds
   removed

1 1/2 teaspoons minced fresh garlic
1 28-ounce (800 g) can tomatoes
2 teaspoons fresh thyme
1 teaspoon fresh basil
1/4 to 1/2 teaspoon white pepper
Salt

Recommended equipment: A medium saucepan, 10-inch (25 cm) cast-iron skillet.

Peel the shrimp, saving the shells. Wash and dry the shrimp and refrigerate; cover the shells with cold water, and bring to simmer. Cook about 15 minutes, strain, and reserve the stock.

Heat the bacon fat in the skillet over medium high heat. Stir in the onion, pepper, and celery, and sauté about 10 minutes, until tender but not brown. Stir in the hot pepper and garlic and cook about 2 minutes. Chop the tomatoes, and add them with their juice to the skillet. Reduce heat and cook at a gentle simmer for at least an hour. As the mixture thickens, add a little shrimp stock from time to time, about 1/2 cup (120 ml) in all. When the flavors are well developed, season with thyme, basil, white pepper and salt.

When ready to serve, bring the mixture up to a good simmer, stir in the reserved shrimp, and cook about 8 to 10 minutes. Serve piping hot with Green Rice (see page 50).

⌬ Shrimp Burgers ⌬

The name is new, but the dish is old. This shrimp mixture has played a number of roles in southern cooking. It may be shaped as little cakes, dipped in bread crumbs, and fried for a first course or served as a garnish for an elaborate entrée. It is baked alone or, with vegetables, as a casserole, or it stuffs large fish such as flounder or red snapper. In Georgetown, South Carolina, drive-ins grill it and put in on a bun with lettuce, tomatoes, and tartar sauce. They advertise their shrimp burgers on hand-painted signs by the road.

Yields 4 servings

1 pound (454 g) cooked shrimp	2½ tablespoons mayonnaise
3 tablespoons diced green pepper	¼ teaspoon dry mustard
2 tablespoons diced celery	1 cup (235 ml) stale bread crumbs
2 tablespoons diced scallions	Salt, pepper, cayenne to taste

Peel the shrimp and chop or grind it roughly. Add the vegetables, mayonnaise, mustard, and bread crumbs. Beat well by hand. Season to taste. If the mixture is for burgers, keep the flavors simple, but if it is for more elegant fare, add lemon or sherry—or both—if desired.

Pork, Beef, and Chicken

Fancy reminds you of the relish with which, at the St. Charles, in New-Orleans, or the Pulaski, in Savannah, or the Charleston Hotel, you have discussed the exquisitely dressed loin, or haunch, done to a turn.

William Gilmore Simms, "Summer Travel in the South," 1850

Pork

"An Inn at Georgetown, S.C. supplied hog and hominy, and corn-cake for breakfast; waffles, hog and hominy for dinner; and hog, hominy, and corn-cake for supper."

So reported the *Knickerbocker Magazine* in 1861, and such was the general impression of eating in the South held by many. Though venison, veal, mutton, and beef were often prepared, pork was the staple meat of the settled South. Only in the warmest areas such as southwestern Louisiana and northern Florida was beef favored, probably due to the lack of success in curing pork in hot climates. These areas still imported cured pork, mostly from Cincinnati, for their demands.

The hog was adaptable to the southern agricultural systems, which did not encourage animal husbandry. A pig could root well in the underbrush, which also provided protection from predators. The forage diet of vines, nuts, and berries only added to the flavor of its flesh. The hog is radically more efficient than cattle or sheep in converting food to flesh; it was therefore much quicker to fatten the rounded-up wild pigs in the fall before slaughter. The lack of developed pasture or forage crops, on the whole, did not hamper swine production as much as that of cattle and sheep.

Slaveholders believed pork much more nutritious than beef and necessarily part of the diet of field workers. Almost every antebellum guide to the care and rations of slaves bears this out. Fresh beef was held so inferior to pork that it was sometimes issued in amounts five times greater than that of pork. That a hog could be raised to maturity in a single season and could be easily preserved made it even more economical from the farmer's point of view.

Fall was and, despite refrigeration, still is the preferred slaughtering time, cool temperatures being necessary for curing the meats. In warmer weather, pork was consumed fresh and sometimes cured in brine, a practice almost forgotten these days, though citizens of New Bern, North Carolina, still prepare corned ham for the winter holidays. For a dry cure the method proposed in 1836 by *The Southern Agriculturist* for a thousand weight of pork is standard, then as now:

Mix one bushel of first rate salt with one pound of saltpetre, rub the pieces well with the mixture, and put them down. In a few days take them up and rub them again, which makes them take the salt evener. In about four weeks, remove them and wash them, when they will be ready to be hung in the smokehouse. . . . The meat should be hung in the smokehouse so that it cannot possibly fall for if a piece should in the fire, it would most probably burn the house. . . . We would add six pounds of brown sugar to every bushel of salt, and in addition we would rub all the parts of a ham where skippers [flies] usually make their attacks, with a small proportion of Cayenne pepper.

Each farmer had his own recipe for cure, which naturally was superior to any other, utilizing ingredients such as black pepper, molasses, wood ashes, bay, and cloves. Hams, shoulders, sidemeat, and jowls were the parts that underwent salt cures. It's said that every part of the hog is used but the oink: the head boiled for head cheese, intestines scraped and boiled for casings or batter-dipped and fried, feet pickled, liver baked for a pudding, brains fried for breakfast with scrambled eggs, every scrap ground for sausage. As in France, ears and tails are considered a delicacy and are displayed in even the most antiseptic modern supermarkets. Fried pork rinds or skins are sold prepackaged and munched on as are potato chips and pretzels in other parts of the country. You will find the same in Mexican markets, where it is called chicharron; it is, in fact, one of the items that assured me of the universality of peasant cooking when I first saw it in the Mercado of Mexico City.

Rendered fresh fat becomes lard for baking short, flaky piecrusts and myriad quick breads. Cured fat cuts come in several forms. Salt pork is simply salt-cured pork fat bought in slabs weighing approximately one pound. The salt must be washed from the surface before using. It is not seasoned or smoked, and is mostly rendered for frying. Streak of lean, pork belly, midlin', sow belly, or sidemeat are essentially the same thing: a seasoned, salt-cured fat cut with at least some lean portion and usually smoked. This cut is used for larding meats and braising vegetables where it gives richness to the potlikker. Hog jowl is leaner yet and may be substituted for sidemeat in braising. Sidemeat in large pieces or jowl when cooked with vegetables is often served separately as a meat dish in poorer households. After the Civil War, even the proudest families were glad to see it.

We spent several months in Columbia after the close of the Confederate War. The struggle for life was very great at that time, yet one never heard a murmur of protest. Everyone tried to pass the time cheerfully. We, the William Ravenels, lived principally on cowpeas and bacon. . . . After finishing our cowpeas, a long time would elapse before Horlsey, our Negro butler, brought the bacon into the room. We became so tired of waiting, wondered why he did not bring in the bacon promptly. . . . One evening I said "Horlsey, why do you wait so long before bringing in the bacon after you take off the soup?" Horlsey looked grave, said "Miss Rose, I am educating you." "Educating me, Horlsey? How?" "Miss Rose, the times are hard. You ought to know how we lived before the war—how things ought to be." Horlsey described a very elaborate dinner with many courses—soup, fish, and game, and so on. He enjoyed instructing me and said, "You must try and think you are eating all those things I mentioned while you are waiting for the bacon." I told Mamma. Thereafter we waited patiently and never found fault at the long interval between cowpeas soup and bacon. (*Rose P. Ravenel's Cookbook*)

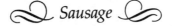# Sausage

When I was growing up, my family always raised a hog or two with my paternal grandparents. I remember clearly the gruesome beginnings and ends—spring castration and fall slaughter. Afterwards, though, there was so much to do I quickly forgot the barbarous scenes; by the time the first shoulders were barbecued, hunger obliterated any sentimental memories of raising tiny pink piglets. Each autumn my grandfather would also grind the sausage, pungent with red pepper and aromatic with sage. Homemade sausage made a special supper on the farm with fried eggs, apples, biscuits, and blackberry jam. Other times, sandwiched in a cold biscuit and carried in a coat pocket, it would sustain my brother and me through the long cold hours of a watchful hunt.

This recipe is an approximation of my grandfather's method—I say method, not recipe, for his process was one of sight and feel, not measurement. Use as much discernment in buying pork and fat as you would in buying fish. In many areas, finding fresh pork fat will be a challenge. Today's pigs are being bred much leaner than in the past; often there isn't enough fat for the demand. European butchers—French, Italian, Portuguese—are usually more willing to work with you than those of the supermarkets. Salt pork, even blanched, will not do, no matter what a meat clerk may tell you. I have heard of, but never tasted, sausage made, in a pinch, with lard.

Yields about 1½ pounds

1 pound (450 g) lean pork, cleaned of all tendons and gristle

½ pound (225 g) fresh pork fat

1½ teaspoons salt

½ teaspoon sugar

¼ teaspoon freshly grated nutmeg

½ teaspoon dried red pepper flakes

¼ teaspoon dried thyme

1 teaspoon dried sage

¾ teaspoon whole black peppercorns

1 to 2 garlic cloves, chopped

1 slice stale bread or a biscuit

Recommended equipment: Mixing bowl, food grinder or grinder attachment for electric mixer, mortar and pestle.

Chop the lean pork and the fresh fat coarsely. Combine in a bowl with the salt, sugar, nutmeg, red pepper flakes, thyme, and sage. Crack the peppercorns roughly in a mortar and pestle and add them as well as

Pork

the garlic. Put all ingredients through the grinder, first using the coarse blade, then the fine blade. You may prefer to use only the coarse blade and grind the mixture three times. After all the sausage has been ground the last time, run a piece of stale bread or biscuit through the grinder to extract all the meat. Lightly work the bread into the rest of the mixture. Shape into patties for frying or stuff into casings (see below) for link sausage.

Note on sausage casings: Natural casings, packed in dry salt, from cattle, sheep, or hogs are available from most butcher shops. The smallest ones are usually used for southern link sausages. To use, wash the casings well, but gently, in cold water. Slip one open end over the water faucet and run cold water through the desired length. Carefully pat dry before using. To stuff, you will need a meat grinder with a sausage horn, or a large pastry bag with a large round tip. Slip the desired length of casing over the horn or tip, and fill gently. Work slowly, but smoothly, avoiding air pockets. Avoid overfilling as well. If you have doubts, fill one or two sausages and cook. If your mixture contains any raw egg, it must be more loosely filled than an all-meat mixture as the egg will expand upon cooking. Use a natural string to separate links. Give the sausage two or three twists before tying. Each end must be securely tied. Most sausages will benefit by 2 days of aging in a cool, dry part of the refrigerator.

❧ *Liver Pudding* ☙

Liver pudding is a dish that one has to be born to. What I mean is that it never appears on restaurant menus, nor is it likely to be served outside the family. Some might say it is too low a dish, too much an economy item to be served to a guest when one can afford more elegant fare, but I suspect it is just too good to waste on anyone who might fail to appreciate its gusto. Sliced and browned, it is too often accompanied by tomato catsup these days, a further mask of its charms. Golden sautéed onions and a slice of lemon will elevate this simple loaf into another realm. Its commercial counterpart runs heavily to cereal and water; this recipe yields a correspondent to the finest regional French charcuterie.

Yields about 20 slices ½ inch (1¼ cm) thick

For the pan

2 tablespoons (30 g) lard
½ teaspoon whole black
   peppercorns
1 bay leaf

½ teaspoon dried thyme
½ teaspoon dried sage
4 whole allspice corns

For the pudding

1¾ pounds (800 g) pork or calf's
   liver, trimmed of all gristle and
   veins, and cut into 1-inch (2½
   cm) cubes
4 ounces (115 g) fresh pork fat,
   finely chopped
2 cups (475 ml) chopped onion
2 eggs
½ cup (118 ml) hot cooking liquid
   from the liver or chicken or
   beef stock

½ cup (118 ml) cornmeal
¾ teaspoon whole black
   peppercorns
¾ teaspoon dried sage
½ teaspoon dried thyme
¼ to ½ teaspoon dried red
   pepper flakes
½ teaspoon freshly grated
   nutmeg
1½ teaspoons salt

For the bain-marie

Boiling water

Recommended equipment: A loaf pan and a larger pan into which it will fit easily, forming a bain-marie; 4-quart (4 L) saucepan; food grinder, food grinder attachment for electric mixer, or food processor; mortar and pestle; aluminum foil; meat thermometer.

Thoroughly grease the interior of the pan with the lard, being sure that all surfaces are coated. Crack all the herbs and spices together in a mortar and pestle until the bay is pulverized. Coat the greased sides and bottom of the loaf pan with the flavorings.

    The liver may be prepared in one of two ways, both of which are used throughout the South. Either precook the liver by covering it with cold water in the saucepan, bringing it to a boil, draining it and reserving ½ cup of the cooking liquid, or grind it raw. In both instances it must be thoroughly cleaned of all gristle and veins before proceeding to the next step.

Preheat oven to 375°F (190°C). Add the liver (raw or cooked) to a bowl in which the pork fat, onion, and eggs are combined. Add the hot stock or cooking liquid to the cornmeal, stir well, and let cool before adding to the liver. Crack the peppercorns roughly in a mortar and pestle, adding them to the bowl along with the sage, thyme, red pepper flakes, nutmeg, and salt. Mix thoroughly and pass through a food grinder (using the fine blade) or a food processor. Pack into the loaf pan and cover tightly with aluminum foil. Set the loaf pan in the larger pan and add 1 inch (2½ cm) of boiling water. Set on the middle level of the preheated oven and bake for about 1 hour if using pre-cooked liver or about 1¾ hours if using raw liver. In either case, the center of the pudding will be set when done, the sides will pull away slightly, and a meat thermometer should read 165°F (72°C).

Let cool at room temperature and turn out of the pan. Wrap well in plastic and refrigerate.

To serve: slice ½ inch (1¼ cm) thick, dredge in flour seasoned with salt and freshly ground black pepper and fry in your preferred fat (bacon, butter, lard, or vegetable oil) until lightly crisp on both sides.

Herb Crust Pork Loin with Onion Gravy

A paste was often employed by English cooks who mastered fine roasting of large cuts and joints of meat. Southern cooks inherited the method and, typically, provided a more piquant seasoning.

Yields 6 to 8 servings

1 center cut loin of pork, on the
    bone, weighing about 4
    pounds (1800 g)

The seasoning paste

2 tablespoons (30 g) butter
1 teaspoon finely chopped garlic
½ cup (61 g) flour
1 teaspoon dried sage
1 teaspoon dried thyme
½ teaspoon red pepper flakes

1 teaspoon dry ground mustard
½ teaspoon sugar
1½ teaspoons salt
¾ teaspoon freshly ground black
    pepper

The sauce

2 cups (475 ml) sliced onion
½ cup (118 ml) stock or water (or
    more if needed during
    roasting)
2 cups (475 ml) stock or water

2½ teaspoons cornstarch
¼ cup (60 ml) sherry
Salt and freshly ground black
    pepper

Recommended equipment: A 10-inch (25 cm) cast-iron skillet or enameled cast-iron sauté pan, roasting pan, 1½-quart (1½ L) heavy-bottomed saucepan, meat thermometer, wire whisk.

Two hours (or more) before cooking, remove the roast from the refrigerator. Trim away excess fat, leaving a ⅛ inch (⅓ cm) covering over the main part of the meat. Dice—*very finely*—enough of the fat to make 2 tablespoons (30 g) and reserve. Across the fleshy part of the roast, cut diagonal slashes ¼ inch (⅔ cm) deep, 1 inch (2½ cm) apart. Repeat in the opposite direction to complete the scoring. Make a similar slash on each side of each rib. Reserve the roast at room temperature.

Prepare the seasoning paste. Render the diced pork fat with the 2 tablespoons of butter in the skillet or sauté pan over low heat. The butter will brown slightly, but do not let it burn. Stir frequently. Add the chopped garlic and stir for 1 minute. Stir in the flour and cook slowly for 3 minutes. Season with the sage, thyme, red pepper flakes, mustard, sugar, salt, and pepper, cooking for 1 minute more. Turn into a bowl and let cool to room temperature.

Rub the roast well with the paste, working it into each cut; the fleshy side should be well coated. Let sit 1½ hours or more, preferably at room temperature.

Preheat the oven to 450°F (232°C).

Scatter the sliced onions evenly over the bottom of the roasting pan. Place the roast on the onions, bone side down. Add the ½ cup stock or water to the pan and place in the middle of the preheated oven. Immediately reduce heat to 325°F (163°C) and roast for about 2½ hours, basting with pan juices every 30 minutes. Add more liquid to the pan as necessary.

When done to 170°F (76°C) on a meat thermometer, remove the roast, carefully, to a serving platter. Pour the onions and liquid from the roasting pan into the saucepan, adding all browned bits of paste or meat from the bottom of the pan. Skim off the fat and add the additional 2 cups of stock or water. Measure the cornstarch into a bowl and stir in the sherry until smooth and free of lumps. Pour in ½ cup (125 ml) of the gravy liquid to dissolve the cornstarch further. Stirring with the whisk, add this mixture to the saucepan and bring to a boil. Taste for salt and pepper, reduce heat to low, and simmer for 10 minutes.

Carve the roast and serve the sauce over the slices. Spoon Bread, Fried Grits, or Grits Croquettes are excellent accompaniments (see pages 29, 31, and 32).

⟰ *Country Ham* ⟱

Hams undergo a variety of cures in the South depending upon the producer. A ham for this recipe may be described as dry-cured with salt, sugar (brown or white), or molasses, and it may have been smoked at some point; but it must be dry cured and never subjected to any sort of brine.

There is always the challenge of what to do with leftover ham. Once cooked, cooled, and refrigerated, a salt-cured ham can easily last a month; there is no rush to dispose of it as with fresh foods. It will also freeze well if wrapped carefully. Bit by bit, though, the delicious flavor can be worked into many dishes. Ground, it flavors soufflés, biscuit dough, sandwich spreads, stuffings for everything from eggs to mushrooms to turkeys. Soups profit enormously from diced ham, as do such rice dishes as paella and jambalaya. The contrast between the elaborately developed flavor of the ham and quickly cooked fresh vegetables such as green beans or cauliflower is always intriguing. Even nonsoutherners can quickly find the country ham becoming a kitchen staple.

Yields enough for a large crowd

1 dry-cured country ham weighing 12 to 15 pounds (5.5 kg to 6.8 kg)
2 changes of water for soaking
2 dried red pepper pods
2 bay leaves
1 tablespoon whole mustard seeds

1 cup (235 ml) apple cider vinegar
2 cups (475 ml) apple cider
1 cup (235 ml) molasses
1½ cups (355 ml) sliced onion
1 cup (235 ml) chopped celery
Water for cooking

Recommended equipment: A 5-gallon (20 L) crock for soaking, 1 stiff brush, 1 very large pot for boiling such as a stockpot or a large canning kettle, roasting pan.

Preparation of the ham
Put the ham into the crock with the hock end (bone end) up. Cover with cold water and soak for 12 hours to remove the salt. Remove ham, discard the water, and scrub the ham all over under running cold water with a stiff, bristle (not metal) brush. Return the ham to the crock and cover it with cold water, soaking it for 12 to 18 more hours.

Cooking the ham
Put the scrubbed, soaked ham into a pot large enough to hold it and add the red pepper, bay leaves, mustard seeds, vinegar, apple cider, molasses, onion, and celery. Add water to cover. Bring to a boil, then reduce heat to a simmer. Begin timing from the boil, and simmer 15 minutes for each pound of the ham's weight. At the end of the cooking time, turn off the heat and allow the ham to cool in its liquid, about 2 hours. Then place it on a large cutting board and remove all the outer skin. Trim the fat to a thickness of ¼ inch (⅔ cm) and shave off any meat directly exposed to the curing agents and any meat that is discolored. As you trim the ham, save any juices (not the poaching stock) exuded by the ham for use in the glaze. If this is the first country ham you have cooked, you may be surprised at the amount of discarded skin, fat, and meat—probably 6 cups at least, but persevere. You will regret leaving any moldy or rancid bits intact for the sake of false economy. After careful trimming, the ham may be served as is, but a glaze will improve it.

Glazing the ham
4 tablespoons light brown sugar
4 tablespoons ground dry
    mustard
4 tablespoons cornmeal
¾ cup (180 ml) ham juices

Preheat oven to 375°F (190°C).
    Combine the sugar, mustard, and cornmeal with the juices from the ham to make a thick paste. Use water or stock (or some white wine or sherry) if you need additional liquid. Put the ham flat side down on a roasting pan. Make long, diagonal slashes ¼ inch (⅔ cm) deep and 1 inch (2½ cm) apart across the surface of the ham. At 90 degrees to these slashes, make additional slashes to form a diamond pattern.

Thickly cover the entire ham with the brown sugar paste (make more paste if needed). Bake in the preheated oven for 30 minutes or until well browned. Let cool at least 30 minutes before carving into paper-thin slices.

ꙮ North Carolina Barbecue Sauce ꙮ

Three meats are called, generically, barbecue in the South. In Virginia and Kentucky, lamb and mutton may fit the category. In the states close to Texas, beef is barbecued. But for most of the South, barbecue means pork, and it is a centuries-old tradition. Barbecue is from the native American tradition, originally a slow-cooking process of any meats or fish over coals. It was known up and down the East coast and recorded by the earliest Spanish explorers of the Caribbean. In seventeenth-century England the barbecue enjoyed a limited vogue after enthusiastic accounts of the technique were reported from early Virginia and Carolina.

A vast literature on the barbecue continues to be written today. This country's leading newspapers, though definitely above the 'cue line, still debate origins, techniques, and sauces. The native origin is documented in early engravings and writings; no state can claim it. The technique for purists is pit cooking—a deep, stone-lined pit filled with hard wood and burned down to coals before the slow cooking begins, despite the intervention of local health departments who favor indoor gas fired furnaces.

The sauces are the most obvious distinctions. The best known nowadays is the western sauce, Texas variety—tomato-based, sweet and sour. This (with artificial smoke flavor added) is what is sold in most grocery stores. Somewhere along the Pee Dee River Basin in South Carolina and on through Georgia, a sweet and pungent mustard sauce is favored. In North Carolina the most traditional sauce is a straightforward mix of vinegar and red pepper. To my taste, it is a classic, hardly interfering with the smoky roast and just setting it off. The ketchup and mustard sauces make a thick, sticky coating. The vinegar sauce gives the roast a crisp coat and cuts the fat.

A true barbecue demands a big piece of meat—half a pig or at least a shoulder—but the method can be adapted to a charcoal grill and a few ribs or a chicken. Just do the initial slow cooking with frequent basting in the oven. Then finish off over the slow coals for 10 minutes on each side.

1 cup (235 ml) apple cider vinegar

$^1/_2$ to $^3/_4$ cup (115 to 175 ml) water

$^2/_3$ cup (160 ml) minced onion

1 garlic clove, crushed

$^1/_2$ teaspoon salt

1 teaspoon ground black pepper

1 to 2 teaspoons red pepper flakes

1 teaspoon sugar

1 bay leaf

$^2/_3$ teaspoon thyme

3 tablespoons peanut oil

2 to 3 teaspoons dry mustard

4 to 6 teaspoons cold water

Recommended equipment: A small stainless steel or enamel saucepan.

Combine all the ingredients except the last two in a small saucepan. Bring to a rapid boil, then simmer five minutes. Remove from heat. Dissolve the mustard in the cold water, then thin it out with some of the hot vinegar sauce. Stir the mustard into the sauce. Let cool, bottle, and store in the refrigerator.

Oven-baked Spareribs

Yields 4 servings

4 pounds (1800 g) pork spareribs

3 quarts (3 L) water

$^1/_2$ cup (115 ml) Barbecue Sauce (see page 102)

$^1/_2$ cup (115 ml) water

More Sauce for basting

Salt and pepper

Recommended equipment: A 6-quart (6 L) pot, baking pan about 11 × 15 inches (27$^1/_2$ × 37$^1/_2$ cm).

Put the spareribs in the pot, cover with cold water, and bring to a boil. Drain and remove to a large bowl.

Pour the barbecue sauce over all sides of the ribs. Pour $^1/_2$ cup water in the bottom of the baking dish and put the ribs on top. Let sit 30 minutes.

Preheat the oven to 300°F (190°C). Roast the ribs until very tender and brown—about 2 hours—basting occasionally. Use more sauce if desired. Season with salt and pepper upon serving. Pass extra sauce with the ribs.

Beef

Only a handful of distinguished beef dishes come from southern kitchens. Judging from the elevation of many more humble food items, one can assume that this was the result of despair at the quality of the meat rather than of any lack of skill on the cook's part. A general neglect of cattle husbandry is described in the *National Register* of 27 July 1816 in a "Topographical and Historical Description of the County of Brunswick, in North Carolina": "Cattle and hogs run wild in the woods, the former are supported in the summer by wild grass, and in the winter by cane rods in swamps. . . . Neither of them ever consume the hay or corn of a farm, until they are intended to be butchered, and then a small quantity of corn or potatoes are given to the hogs."

The importance of cash cropping on the large plantations was one factor that limited development of pasturage. Cleared land was given over to the production of the enormously profitable export crops of tobacco, rice, indigo and, later, cotton. Not only pasturage was thwarted; hay and forage crops were neglected as well. The want of animal confinement led to other problems in cattle production—with no penning there was no control over breeding and thus no line improvement. Similarly, no dairy cow lines were established; lactating females provided the only milk. In many parts of the South, cattle reverted to a feral state and were shot as game. Herders of cattle usually lived alone in temporary shacks on the outskirts of civilization. The cattle were brought to pens in the spring for branding of the young and driving the mature animals to market. One of these sites in up-country South Carolina gained lasting fame as the site of an important Revolutionary War skirmish, the Battle of Cowpens.

In the antebellum period, most beef was eaten fresh because its cure was more precarious than that for pork. When preserved, it was usually pickled in brine. The Reverend Woodmason noted another technique: "If any Beef they jerk it and dry it in the Sun." Summer was the main season for beef consumption—cattle were fatter from the fresh grass and the store of preferred cured pork of the previous fall was exhausted. The most famous and best traditional beef dish is a variation on a French summer dish—the Boeuf en Daube Glacé. Despite a general lack of enthusiasm for cold meats in aspic in the United

States, this daube is found in various guises in every state from Maryland to Louisiana on summer menus. A gentle braising is the basis of most other southern beef dishes as well, including country-style steak and grillades, for the likely tough and lean flesh. The advantage is a full and complex accompanying gravy.

∾ *Country Style Steak* ∾

Yields 6 to 8 servings

1½ teaspoons freshly ground
   black pepper
¾ teaspoon dried thyme
¾ teaspoon dried sage
¼ teaspoon salt
¼ teaspoon red pepper flakes
2½ pounds (1125 g) lean beef
   steaks, such as round, ½ inch
   (1¼ cm) thick

3 slices bacon, cut into 1-inch
   (2½ cm) squares
Peanut oil or lard, if needed
6 tablespoons flour
1 teaspoon salt
4 cups (950 ml) sliced onions
2 garlic cloves, chopped
½ teaspoon sugar
3 cups (710 ml) cold water or beef
   stock

Recommended equipment: A 10-inch (25 cm) cast-iron skillet or enameled cast-iron sauté pan.

Combine the pepper, thyme, sage, salt, and red pepper flakes in a bowl and rub the steaks well all over with the mixture. Set aside to season for at least 20 minutes, preferably overnight, covered, in the refrigerator.

    Render the bacon in the skillet or sauté pan until it browns. Remove the bacon, drain, and set aside. If necessary add fat to the pan for browning the steaks. Combine the flour and salt on a plate and dredge the steaks, reserving the remaining flour for thickening the gravy. Over medium heat brown the beef well on each side and reserve the steaks. Add the onions and garlic and sauté over low heat until tender. Sprinkle with the sugar and the remaining flour. Stir in well, raise heat to medium, and cook until golden. Add the water or stock slowly, stirring constantly. Return the steaks and bacon to the pan and simmer for 40 minutes or until very tender.

∾ *Grillades and Grits* ∾

Grillades and grits is about the most delicious, most hearty breakfast I know of. Working-class Creoles and Cajuns of Louisiana have relied on it for years to supply the energy for the day's work. No matter when it is consumed—for the more sedentary of us it is an excellent brunch or supper dish—it is to be relished.

    A grillade is a square-cut piece of lean meat fried and often served with a sauce. These grillades are much more—a reflection of the innate understanding a Cajun cook has of his ingredients. After frying, the steaks are slowly simmered in a classic Cajun-style sauce until the moment that the flavors reach their ultimate development and the meat becomes its most tender—perfection in timing.

Yields 4 servings

1 pound 4 ounces (575 g) lean beef, veal, or pork steaks, ½ inch (1¼ cm) thick
¼ cup (60 ml) flour
½ teaspoon salt
½ teaspoon freshly ground black pepper
2 tablespoons (30 g) bacon fat or lard
1½ cups (355 ml) sliced onion
½ cup (118 ml) chopped celery
1 cup (235 ml) chopped red or green bell pepper
2 garlic cloves, minced
2 tablespoons bacon fat or lard
2 tablespoons flour

1½ cups (355 ml) sliced fresh, ripe tomato
1¼ cups (295 ml) water or stock
1 teaspoon dried thyme
½ teaspoon dried basil
½ teaspoon red pepper flakes (or more)
¼ cup (60 ml) Pepper Sauce (see page 147) or vinegar
Salt and freshly ground black pepper
2 tablespoons chopped, fresh parsley
4½ cups Basic Boiled Grits (see page 30)

Recommended equipment: A 12-inch (30 cm) cast-iron skillet or enameled cast-iron sauté pan.

Cut the steaks into 2-inch (5 cm) squares. Mix the flour, salt, and pepper and dredge the steaks. Heat the bacon fat in the skillet or sauté pan over high heat and sauté the meat on each side, browning well. Remove the meat to a holding dish, leaving the fat behind in the pan.

Sauté the onion, celery, and pepper in the same pan until tender. Add garlic and stir well. Push the vegetables to one side of the pan. Add the additional 2 tablespoons of bacon fat and stir in the 2 tablespoons of flour. Stir the roux well and cook until it turns a rich medium brown. Add the water or stock and stir all until smooth.

Return the meat to the pan and scatter the tomatoes over all. Season with thyme, basil, red pepper flakes, and the Pepper Sauce or vinegar. Reduce heat to a simmer and cook until tender, about 40 to 60 minutes, depending upon the type of meat used. Taste for salt and

Beef

pepper and stir in the 2 tablespoons of chopped parsley. Serve over hot, well-buttered grits.

∾ *Boeuf en Daube Glacé* ∾

Yields 10 to 12 servings

The stock

2 pounds (900 g) pork neck bones, cut in 2-inch (5 cm) sections
2 pounds (900 g) beef or veal shanks, cut in 1-inch (2½ cm) sections
2 pair pig's feet, split
2 pair calf's feet, split
2 tablespoons peanut oil
2 cups (475 ml) chopped celery

2 cups (475 ml) chopped carrots
4 cups (1 L) chopped onions
2 teaspoons dried thyme
½ teaspoon red pepper flakes
2 bay leaves
6 whole cloves
3 teaspoons salt
20 whole black peppercorns
4 quarts (4 L) cold water

The beef

1 lean bottom round of beef, weighing about 4 pounds (1800 g)

1 large or 2 small garlic cloves
2 ounces (60 g) pork sidemeat
2 tablespoons vegetable oil

Final seasoning

¼ cup (60 ml) dry sherry
½ cup (118 ml) thinly sliced scallions

¼ cup (60 ml) chopped fresh parsley
1 tablespoon chopped fresh tarragon (optional)

Garnishes: hard-boiled eggs; lemon wedges; radishes; tomato wedges; watercress; whole scallions; heart of celery ribs

Recommended equipment: A roasting pan, 8-quart (8 L) stockpot with lid, 12-inch (30 cm) cast-iron skillet or enameled cast-iron sauté pan, ladle for skimming, strainer, thin-bladed knife such as a boning knife, two mixing bowls, 3-quart (3 L) mold or two loaf pans.

Procedure for the stock
Preheat the oven to 450°F (232°C).

Scatter all the meats and bones in the roasting pan, place on the middle rack of the oven and brown well, turning to ensure equal cooking. In the bottom of the stockpot heat the oil and sauté the vegetables until lightly browned. Add thyme, red pepper flakes, bay, cloves, salt, and peppercorns. Add meats when well browned, including any drippings. Cover with cold water and bring to a boil over high heat. Skim the stock, reduce the heat and simmer for 4 to 5 hours, removing any protein scum or fat which rises to the surface of the broth periodically throughout the cooking.

When meat and bones are thoroughly cooked and stock is well flavored, strain the liquid, discarding the solids. Return the stock to the pot and reduce to 8 cups (1900 ml), still skimming. Reserve in the stockpot.

Procedure for the beef
Trim the beef of any excess exterior fat. With a sharply pointed knife (or swivel-bladed vegetable peeler) make 30 evenly spaced 1½ inch (3¾ cm) deep incisions into the meat on all sides. Chop the garlic with the pork sidemeat into a rough paste, and pack some of this paste into each incision. Heat the 2 tablespoons of oil in the skillet or sauté pan and brown the beef well on all sides. Add the beef to the reduced stock, cover, and simmer about 3 hours or until tender.

Final assembly
Remove the beef from the stock and set aside until cool enough to handle. Meanwhile, carefully skim the stock of all fat, strain and measure. You will need approximately 6 cups (1400 ml) for the aspic. Add sherry and taste for salt and pepper. Put a small amount of the stock in a cold teacup and refrigerate. When cold it should set up as an aspic. If it fails to set up, dissolve ½ tablespoon unflavored gelatin in ½ cup (118 ml) warm stock. Stir back into the remaining stock and test again. If any more gelatin is required, add it in very small increments.

When beef is cool, shred it by pulling apart with two forks. Toss with the scallions and parsley (and tarragon if desired). Cool the aspic by stirring it in a mixing bowl set over another bowl filled with ice water. When it begins to thicken, fold in the beef. Pour into the mold or two loaf pans. Refrigerate well—at least 6 to 8 hours—before serving.

To serve, dip the mold into a pan full of warm water. Quickly run a knife around the edges of the mold and invert onto a serving dish. Surround with the desired garnishes and slice to serve.

Calvin Trillin in his chronicles of culinary America has done as much to champion cholesterol as Nathan Pritikin with his famous diet has to combat it. The two, metaphorically, came head-to-head when Trillin traveled to Natchitoches, Louisiana, to report on an attempt to switch the dietary allegiances of the populace to the stark Pritikin regime as part of a medical study. The result was a foregone conclusion "in Cajun country, where people's main interest in an old building tends to be what sort of food might be served in it" *(Third Helpings)*. Louisiana's Governor Edwards told Trillin that Pritikin would have found it easier to convert people in "other parts of the country where the food is no good anyway." It would be unforgivable to renounce a tradition such as the Natchitoches meat pie. These empanada-like pastries, once sold by young blacks, are a rare example of street food in the South. They are now prepared and sold from stands at festival times such as Christmas and the grand homes pilgrimage.

The dough is soft and must be refrigerated throughout the preparation to prevent tearing. It also cooks extremely quickly; be on guard for burning. Preparation may be done in stages, and once filled, the pies may rest refrigerated for as much as an hour if both pastry and meat are cold. As with all fried foods, serve immediately upon cooking. Smaller meat pies make a good hot hors d'oeuvre; larger ones, with cold beer, make an ideal supper for TV football marathons. These are excellent served with Cajun Tomato Sauce (see page 147).

Yields 16 pies

Spiced meat filling

½ pound (225 g) lean beef chuck
½ pound (225 g) lean pork
1½ tablespoons (23 g) lard
½ cup (118 ml) finely chopped onion
¼ cup (60 ml) finely chopped celery
¼ cup (60 ml) finely chopped green pepper

1 teaspoon minced garlic
¼ teaspoon freshly ground black pepper
¼ teaspoon (or more) ground cayenne pepper
½ teaspoon paprika
1 teaspoon sugar
½ teaspoon dried thyme
1¼ teaspoons salt

Beef

1½ tablespoons flour
¼ cup (60 ml) water
1 cup (235 ml) chopped, fresh
    tomato

Recommended equipment: A 12-inch (30 cm) cast-iron skillet or enameled cast-iron sauté pan, large knife for mincing, rolling pin, frying thermometer.

Chop both the beef and pork by hand very finely, removing any excess fat and membrane. Heat the lard in the skillet or sauté pan until almost smoking. Add the chopped meat and stir frequently over high heat until lightly browned. Add the vegetables, cooking until just tender. Then add the seasonings: garlic, both peppers, paprika, sugar, thyme, and salt. Continue cooking until excess liquid evaporates, add flour and stir well, cooking for 4 or 5 more minutes. Stir in the water and tomato, simmering for 10 to 15 minutes, or until the meat is tender. Turn into a bowl, set aside and chill.

Pastry

2 cups (244 g) flour
2 teaspoons baking powder
1 teaspoon salt

6 tablespoons (90 g) lard
2 eggs
2 tablespoons water

Sift the flour, baking powder, and salt into a mixing bowl. Cut in the lard quickly until the mixture resembles coarse cornmeal. Beat the eggs with the water and stir into the flour mixture with a few rapid strokes. Form into a rectangle 1 × 8 × 12 inches (2½ × 20 × 30 cm), sprinkle with flour, and wrap in plastic wrap or waxed paper. Refrigerate for 40 minutes.

Assembly and cooking

Flour for rolling out pastry
Iced water in a bowl
1 cup (235 ml) peanut oil,
    shortening, or lard for frying

Cut the pastry dough into 16 pieces, refrigerating all but one. Sprinkle a clean, dry counter or pastry marble with flour and shape the piece of dough into a circle about 4 inches (10 cm) in diameter. Lightly dampen the outer edges of the circle with the cold water. Place 1½ to 2 table-spoons of the spiced meat in the center. Quickly fold the pastry in half, sealing the edges with the tines of a fork. Cut away the ragged edges. Chill. Repeat procedure until all the pies are formed.

Heat the fat in the clean skillet or sauté pan to 360°F (182°C). Fry each pie until golden on each side: this will take less time than you expect. Serve immediately with Cajun Tomato Sauce (see page 147).

Chicken

When my grandmother wanted chicken and dumplings, my sister and I were sent to do battle in the hen yard. Brandishing little rods with crookneck ends, we felt like Roman soldiers among the Sabines. In wild pursuit, we ran in a crouch, with our garnering weapons outstretched to catch the hooks around a leg of the prey. Success depended upon tripping the hen up with a jerk of the left hand while grabbing its feet quickly with the right hand. Squawking and head down, the hen was received by my waiting grandmother, who dispatched it with a quick wring of the neck. Of course, no battle was ever so smooth as in its retelling; though old and fat, the barnyard birds found new agility in impending doom. Just when I would put my energy into a quick yank, the old hen would hop to a short flight—I'd be pulling at air and find myself quickly head over heels in a cloud of dust.

Most southern chicken recipes are based on mature fowl, too old to be of much value as laying hens. Only a long, slow simmering could make them tender. Young birds were more valuable for eggs than for their flesh. The tender frying chicken was as great a rarity and luxury as is the whitest veal today.

Poached Chicken

1 chicken weighing about
   4 pounds (1800 g)
1 medium onion, chopped
3 ribs of celery, chopped
⅛ teaspoon red pepper flakes

2 bay leaves
1 teaspoon thyme
2 teaspoons salt
12 whole black peppercorns
2 quarts (2 L) water

Recommended equipment: An 8-quart (8 L) stockpot.

Wash the chicken under cold running water and drain in a colander. Combine the onion, celery, red pepper flakes, bay, thyme, salt, peppercorns, and water in the stockpot. Bring rapidly to a boil over high heat. Carefully add the chicken and return to the boil. Immediately reduce heat to low (the barest simmer) and poach about 90 minutes in all. Do not overcook. If the skin pulls away from the leg joints, it is done.

Remove the chicken from the broth, reserving both for another recipe. When cool enough to handle, remove the meat from the bone.

Chicken Country Captain

Miss Leslie's New Cookery Book of 1857 describes the origin of chicken country captain: "This is an East India dish and a very easy preparation of curry. The term 'Country Captain' signifies a captain of the native troops (or Sepoys) in the pay of England; their own country being India, they are there called generally the country troops. Probably this dish was first introduced at English tables by a Sepoy officer."

This dish is so thoroughly naturalized now in the South that I have heard its birthright claimed by an inhabitant of almost every large seaport. The seaports transmitted the exotic spices to the cooks of the South, so that any dish featuring cinnamon, nutmeg, ginger, or curry—the flavorings of the Indies and the Orient—was associated with the major harbor towns. Today, the great spice houses and Old Bay seasoning itself are symbols of Baltimore.

The curry powder for country captain was most likely a homemade compound. Mrs. Mary Randolph printed her recipe in the *Virginia Housewife* in 1831: "One ounce Turmeric, one do. [ditto] Coriander Seed, one do. Cummin Seed, one do. white ginger, one of nutmeg, one of mace, and one of *Cayenne* pepper; pound all together, and pass through a fine Sieve; bottle and cook it well—one Teaspoonful is sufficient to season any made Dish."

Below is another combination you may want to try. Historically, curry powders were invented in India for the European market, and do not exist as such for native cooks, each Indian dish calling for its own combination of flavors. You may build a base such as the one below and then vary it to suit the demands of different dishes—adding stronger flavors for meats, emphasizing more delicate ones for fish or vegetables.

Black pepper—2 parts by weight
Red pepper—4 parts by weight
Cloves—$\frac{1}{2}$ part by weight
Cardamom—1 part by weight
Coriander—6 parts by weight
Cumin—4 parts by weight
Turmeric—4 parts by weight

Use whole corns or seeds of black pepper, cloves, cardamom, cumin; lightly toast the coriander seeds before grinding. Use whole dried red cayenne pods for the red pepper. (Cinnamon, ginger, fenu-greek, mustard, nutmeg, and allspice may be incorporated as well.) Whole fresh spices ground quickly in a blender or food processor will yield a richer taste than can ever be bought off a shelf. When you do buy a commercial mix, buy the very best. Otherwise you will be paying top dollar for little more than turmeric and fenugreek.

When seeking a curry taste, remember that it takes both time and heat to fully develop both flavor and color. I like to make country captain with the boned meat from a small hen so it can be reheated successfully. Chicken on the bone cooks too quickly to fully interact with the sauce; cooled and then reheated, the young, undeveloped flesh of today's fryers breaks down, tastes musty and bloody at the bone. A firmer, more mature bird will stand up better to the test of the sauce, and will reward you with irresistible leftovers.

Yields 8 to 10 servings

1 chicken weighing about 4
    pounds (1800 g), poached
    (see page 114)

The sauce

1½ ounces (45 g) pork sidemeat, diced to make 2½ tablespoons
1 tablespoon peanut oil
1 28-ounce (800 g) can tomatoes, chopped with juice to make 3 cups
2 cups (475 ml) thinly sliced onion
2 cups (475 ml) thinly sliced green bell pepper
2 large garlic cloves, chopped (to equal 1½ teaspoons)

1¼ teaspoons dried thyme
3 to 5 teaspoons "hot" curry powder or your own spice mixture
¼ teaspoon red pepper flakes
1 cup (235 ml) chicken stock, reserved from Poached Chicken
½ teaspoon freshly ground black pepper
⅓ cup (80 ml) dried currants

The rice and garnish

2¾ cups (655 ml) chicken stock, reserved from Poached Chicken
1¼ cups (295 ml) raw long grain rice

Salt
½ cup (118 ml) slivered almonds, toasted
Freshly chopped parsley

Recommended equipment: A 3-quart (3 L) heavy-bottomed saucepan with lid, 1½-quart (1½ L) saucepan with lid.

While the chicken is poaching, put the peanut oil in the larger saucepan and over low heat render the finely diced pork sidemeat for 10 minutes, stirring frequently.

Meanwhile drain the tomatoes, reserving the juice in a bowl. Chop the tomatoes and return them to the bowl with juice and set aside.

Add the onion to the pork, stir, cover, and cook for 5 minutes. Stir in the bell pepper, re-cover, and cook an additional 5 minutes. Uncover, add the garlic, thyme, curry powder, and red pepper flakes. Raise heat to medium and cook for 3 minutes, stirring well and frequently. Add the tomatoes with the reserved chicken stock to the vegetable mixture. Bring to a boil, reduce heat, and simmer for 15 minutes, still stirring frequently.

In the small saucepan, bring the 2¾ cups of chicken stock to a boil. Add the rice and salt, and return to the boil. Cover, reduce heat to low, and cook for 25 minutes, stirring occasionally.

As soon as the rice is cooking on low, roughly chop the reserved chicken (you should have approximately 3½ to 4 cups or 825 to 950 ml) and add it to the vegetables and stock. Stir in the dried currants and simmer for 20 minutes.

To serve, put the rice around a large platter. Ladle the chicken into the middle. Garnish the rice with the fresh chopped parsley and sprinkle the toasted almonds over the chicken.

ҩ Chicken with Green Dumplings ҩ

While growing up, I always thought of chicken and dumplings as a rustic farm dish. Perhaps it was just the lack of euphony in the word dumpling—phonics have ruined the reputation of more than one dish. Yet the balance of a perfectly poached bird napped in a mushroom sauce and garnished with savory, fresh herb pillows is worthy of the most elegant menus.

Yields 8 to 10 servings

1 chicken weighing about 4
   pounds (1800 g), poached (see
   page 114)

The sauce

8 tablespoons (118 ml) chicken fat
1 cup (235 ml) chopped onion
2 cups (475 ml) chopped fresh
   mushrooms
1 garlic clove, minced
9 tablespoons flour

6 cups (1410 ml) chicken stock
½ cup (118 ml) heavy cream
Salt and freshly ground black
   pepper
12 drops Tabasco sauce

Recommended equipment: A 5-quart (5 L) heavy-bottomed saucepan with lid.

Heat the chicken fat over medium heat in the saucepan. Add the onion and sauté until translucent. Add the mushrooms and continue cooking until the moisture evaporates, about 7 minutes. Stir in the garlic and cook for 2 minutes. Make a roux by adding all the flour at once and stir continuously for 3 minutes. The flour will take on color from the mushrooms; do not let it brown from the heat.

Pour in the stock and cream, stirring continuously, and simmer for 15 minutes. Roughly chop the reserved chicken, add it to the stock, and simmer 15 more minutes. Season well with salt, pepper, and Tabasco sauce. Prepare the dumpling batter.

The dumplings

1½ cups (183 g) flour
2 teaspoons baking powder
1 teaspoon salt
1 teaspoon sugar
1 egg well beaten, with enough milk added to equal ⅞ cup (205 ml)

2 tablespoons chopped, fresh basil or 1 tablespoon dried
2 tablespoons chopped, fresh parsley
4 tablespoons chopped scallions (green and white parts)

Sift the flour, baking powder, salt, and sugar together twice. Make a well in the center of the dry ingredients and quickly stir in all the liquid. Gently fold in the herbs and scallions.

Drop by large spoonfuls into the simmering broth with chicken. The dumplings can be very close together. Cover tightly immediately, and reduce heat so liquid bubbles, but does not boil. Cook 10 minutes or until tender.

To serve, place the chicken in its sauce in the center of a large, heated serving platter. Garnish around the edges with the herb dumplings.

Buttermilk Sage Dumplings

Another dumpling is a rolled pastry, a biscuit dough treated rather like a fat German egg noodle. Prepare the chicken and sauce as above, or for a plainer dish, omit the mushrooms and cream. These dumplings are delicious reheated.

Yields 6 servings

2 cups (244 g) flour
1 teaspoon salt
1½ teaspoons baking powder
1 teaspoon baking soda

¼ teaspoon black pepper
4 tablespoons butter or lard
1 teaspoon fresh, chopped sage
¾ cup (180 ml) buttermilk

Sift the dry ingredients together. Work in the fat until the mixture resembles coarse meal as for biscuits. Add the sage and stir in the buttermilk. Turn out onto a lightly floured surface and knead about 15 strokes, more so than for biscuits. Roll thinly, about ⅛ inch (⅓ cm) thick. Cut into rectangles about 1 × 2 inches.

Drop into the boiling broth, cover and cook about 5 to 7 minutes.

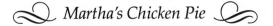 ## Martha's Chicken Pie

This recipe comes from my friend Martha Collett who lives in New York but thinks and eats in the South. It is well known in Morganton, North Carolina, where Martha hails from, and it is typical of the southern chicken pie, which is not a pot pie. The southern version has only a top crust and doesn't admit the array of vegetables found in Yankee versions.

A chicken pie is not exactly fancy food, but it is company food, especially in the fall and winter. It is also for special family dinners, as most cooks who prepare it take more than ordinary pride in their presentation. It is one of those dishes by which cooks are judged, for its simplicity betrays any error in execution or excess in judgment.

Martha doesn't do this, but I do: poach the gizzard and heart with the chicken, and dice; sauté the liver, dice, and add all giblets to the sauce. No one will ever know they're there, but everyone will say it tastes like chicken used to.

Yields 6 servings

1 chicken weighing about 4
   pounds (1800 g), poached (see
   page 114)

The crust

1 cup (122 g) flour
¼ teaspoon salt
½ cup (122 g) butter
2½ tablespoons cold water

The sauce

3 tablespoons butter
3 tablespoons flour
1 cup (235 ml) stock

1 cup (235 ml) milk
2 tablespoons butter

1 cup (235 ml) thinly sliced
  mushrooms
Salt, white pepper, cayenne

1 tablespoon fresh, chopped
  parsley
Butter for the pan

Recommended equipment: A 9-inch (23 cm) pie pan, medium-size saucepan, small skillet.

Bone the chicken when it is cool, and chop the meat into 1-inch squares. Reserve.

Sift the flour and salt together. Cut in the butter until the mixture resembles meal. Quickly stir in the cold water, turn out onto a floured surface, and knead lightly 3 or 4 strokes. Form into a 5-inch (12.5 cm) circle, wrap, and refrigerate for at least 30 minutes.

Melt 3 tablespoons butter in the saucepan, stir in the flour, and cook over medium low heat for 3 minutes. Slowly stir in the stock and milk, bring to a boil, and simmer. Melt 2 tablespoons butter in a small skillet. When hot, sauté the mushrooms quickly, about 3 or 4 minutes. Add the mushrooms to the sauce, stir in the chicken, and season well with salt, pepper, and cayenne. Add the parsley and remove from heat.

Preheat oven to 400°F (204°C).

Butter a 9-inch (23 cm) pie pan well. Pour in the chicken mixture. Roll out the pastry into a circle to fit the top of the pie, and place it over the chicken mixture, crimping the edges. Cut in several steam vents. Place on the middle rack of the preheated oven. After 15 minutes, reduce heat to 350°F (177°C). Continue baking for a total cooking time of 60 minutes or until the crust is crisp and golden. Remove from oven to a rack and let set up 15 minutes before serving.

❧ Southern Fried Chicken with Country Gravy ❧

Southern fried chicken is the center of more controversies than perhaps any other item of food. Some people will tell you to remove the skin before battering, some swear by a double-dip in batter. There is chicken fried in oil, in butter, in shortening, in lard, and in bacon grease. Some poor birds are saturated with all sorts of foreign elements, from Worcestershire to soy sauce. Now, what makes southern fried chicken a classic is its perfect combination of raw material and technique. You want chicken that tastes like chicken, with a crust that snaps and breaks with fragility—a contrast to the tender, moist meat.

No detail can be overlooked without spoiling the integrity of your bird, so be patient and careful. Scrutinize every aspect of the job, and a perfectly fried chicken will unfold itself. No new tricks or magic seasonings can improve its beautiful simplicity.

First, the bird: only a whole, fresh chicken will do. (Frozen chicken tastes bloody and turns dark at the bone when fried. If you find yourself in the possession of one, stew it or bury it.) Wash it well under running cold water and let it dry. Then, and always, cut the bird into nine pieces, that is, with a wishbone—southerners call it the "pulley-bone." Fried chicken without a wishbone is like a life without a childhood, so resign yourself to a little butcher work.

To find this amuletic morsel, press firmly with your fingertips the meat at the neck end of the breasts. The wishbone connects these two muscles, rising from a base on each side near the wing joint to a small but protruding knob. Cut behind the knob with a sharp pointed boning knife down to the base on either side, with plenty of meat attached. (Take care to preserve the magic and avoid cracking the bones.) Disjoint the remaining carcass so you have two wings, two thighs, and two legs. In all these separations, find the actual joints and work the knife between them. Do not cut, hack, or splinter any bones or you might as well buy packaged parts. Detach the whole breast from the backbone by running through the fragile ribs and snapping it at the neck end. Then split the breasts as cleanly as possible through the septum.

Second, the pan: A heavy cast-iron skillet is the only *authentic* implement (an enameled cast-iron skillet is an acceptable substitute). Go to a good, old-fashioned hardware store and buy one if you don't already have it. Gourmet and cooking stores do not generally carry them. To fry a whole chicken in one batch, buy one 12 inches (30 cm) in diameter with a lid to match. Take it home and wash it, for this *one time only,* in hot water, *no* soap. Dry it immediately and place it on a burner. Pour in ½ inch (1 cm) of vegetable oil and turn the burner to a low heat. Season the pan for 40 minutes, periodically oiling the inside walls with a natural bristle pastry brush. Discard the oil and cool the pan, wiping it well with paper towels. Never wash this pan again—over the years it will blacken with use, and, if necessary, can be scoured with a small amount of salt. Soaps, detergents, and metal pads will destroy the patina you want to nurture. Now that you have a pan and the know-how to butcher your bird, get ready to cook.

Yields 4 servings

1 chicken weighing 3 to 3½
  pounds (1350–1575 g), cut into
  9 pieces
1 cup (235 ml) buttermilk
1 cup (235 ml) all-purpose flour

1 teaspoon salt
½ teaspoon black pepper
1 cup (225 g) lard
1½ cups (355 ml) peanut oil

Recommended equipment: A boning knife, medium mixing bowl, 12-inch (30 cm) cast-iron skillet with cover (see introduction above), frying thermometer, two paper bags, wooden whisk.

Put the chicken pieces in a glass or stainless steel bowl and toss with the buttermilk. Let marinate for at least 2 hours. Combine the flour, salt, and pepper in a large paper bag and preheat the lard and peanut oil in the skillet to medium high (375°F or 190°C). Drop the chicken pieces into the paper bag, shaking well to coat them evenly with the seasoned flour. Add the dark pieces to the fat first, skin side down, followed by the white pieces. Reduce heat to medium, cover, and fry 15 minutes. Remove cover, turn each piece, and fry another 10 to 15 minutes uncovered. Remove chicken to the second paper bag to drain and prepare the gravy.

2 tablespoons fat plus drippings
  from the pan
½ cup (100 g) raw country ham
  cut in julienne strips

2 tablespoons of the seasoned
  flour
2 cups (475 ml) whole milk or
  buttermilk

Slowly pour all but 2 tablespoons of cooking fat from the skillet, being careful to leave behind all of the browned flour drippings in the bottom of the pan. Over moderate heat stir in the country ham and cook for 3 minutes. Add flour and stir constantly with a whisk until the flour is well browned—do not scorch. Gradually add the milk or buttermilk, stirring all the while, and bring to a gentle boil for 5 minutes. Serve over rice or biscuits, but not over the chicken.

Tomato Gravy for Fried Chicken

Tomato gravy is less frequently encountered than milk gravy, but it makes a delicious variation in the summer. Pork chops may be fried in much the same way as chicken and are well accompanied by this sauce.

Yields about 2 cups

2 tablespoons fat plus drippings from the pan
1/4 cup (60 ml) minced onion
2 tablespoons of the seasoned flour
2 cups (475 ml) tomatoes (blanched, peeled, and seeded; see page xiv), chopped

Chicken stock or water
1/2 teaspoon dried thyme
1 teaspoon sugar
Salt and freshly ground black pepper

Recommended equipment: A 12-inch (30 cm) cast-iron skillet used for frying the chicken.

In the skillet, sauté the minced onion in the 2 tablespoons of fat until lightly browned. Stir in the flour and cook until it is well browned. Add the chopped tomatoes and stir well. Chicken stock or water may be needed, depending on the amount of liquid yielded by the tomatoes. Season with thyme, sugar, salt, and pepper. Simmer for 30 minutes and serve very hot with the chicken and biscuits or rice (or with other meats such as chops or steaks).

Game

I do not think I ever saw as many wild birds gathered together as in the early winter of 1863. The Combahee raid had swept away the negroes from the river after the crop was planted, and the rice had ripened and fallen at its own will. Perhaps the early migrants among the ducks had sent wireless messages to their friends in Canada, or perhaps the huge flocks passing over looked down at the land and thought it good. Whatever the cause they swarmed there in countless thousands. A wild duck is a very smart "proposition." They can calculate to a nicety how far a fowling piece can carry, and then will cover the expanse of a flowed field, leaving along the banks just the necessary width of clear water. It is only when a young bird gets bossy and knows better than his daddy that you can bushwhack him from the bank. When I took Ross Davis to Myrtle Grove to show him more birds in one place than he had ever seen separately in one place in his life, this very thing happened. A fool duck thought he would see what uniform Ross wore, so he edged in towards us. Ross grabbed my gun! Bang! The duck was dead! And Ross reared up his tall figure as if to invite my admiration of that figure as well as of his shooting. But his face fell as I asked how he was going to retrieve that duck. We had never a dog and never a boat. Ross swore he would never leave *his* duck—shot, mind you, on *Mr. Heyward's land* with *my* gun. There was no help for it! Off came his uniform! Off came lots of other things, until Ross stood up in the altogether.

And the day was cold, and a fierce northwest wind blew, coming from the land whence came Sherman's hard heart! A skim of ice lay upon the water where the banks gave shelter. In Ross plunged boldly, wading where he might and swimming where he must, and thus brought out his duck. Dripping and shivering he drew clothing over his "demned moist" but pleasant body, and smiled cheerfully as I suggested a quick walk and some of that old brandy. Man is a funny creature! All this for one little duck when I would have given him a dozen out of Cook Renty's larder. But then, though a poor thing, it was his own!

How I love to let my thoughts linger over those weeks, for they were like a bookmark between the happy chapters of a dying past, and the lurid pages of a tragic future. Within a year poor Ross was to add his life to a thousand others, sacrificed in vain to repel invasion of their country and to guard their firesides; for he fell before Petersburg, shot through the heart.

D. E. Huger Smith, *A Charlestonian's Recollections*

The annual ritual of the hunt is inaugurated each fall in the southern states, the young quail, rabbit, and deer reaching maturity and fattening on ripening berries, persimmons, and nuts. The native Americans knew and freely hunted a much wider variety of game than hunters do today. The Timucuan Indians of northern Florida impaled alligators on long poles thrust down their throats. Passenger pigeons roosted in such numbers that they could be knocked from the trees at night—a coincidence which saved the French Huguenots at Fort Caroline, who were on the brink of starvation before the flocks arrived. And buffalo, which until recently faced extinction, once roamed Tennessee and Kentucky in large herds.

Conservation efforts have brought the recently rare white-tailed deer back in great numbers. Formerly the staple meat of frontier settlers and undoubtedly the single most important source of animal protein for the American Indians, who often trapped them by setting fires, these animals weigh from 50 to 350 pounds and once traveled in herds numbering two hundred or more. The black bear was also extremely important in the diet of the natives and early settlers, primarily for the huge reserves of fat it carried. This fat was the single most important source of cooking and domestic oil in the wilderness and frontier. An interview from *Foxfire* magazine reveals the ongoing appreciation for the most powerful animal in the southeastern forests:

Every man that we talked to said that one of the biggest reasons for bear hunting, besides the excitement of the hunt, was the taste of the meat itself. And each had his own way of cooking it.

Jerald Cogdill said, "We cut the bear meat up into chunks, put it in the pot, and parboil it. Chop up all the parts of the bear and mix it up and parboil it until it starts getting pretty good and tender. Then just add potatoes and peas and all that good stuff in there. By the time your potatoes get cooked, your meat's good and tender. It takes about five hours to make a big pot of stew. It takes a pretty good while unless you've got a pressure cooker to cook it in. I like it that way. I don't like roast too good myself."

Bear Hunter said, "It's worth every penny it costs me to get one. I really like the meat. I can eat it three times a day and then between meals. Now if you want something good, take a piece of it and cook it of a night. Say you're going tomorrow: put it in a biscuit, wrap it up in a piece of paper, and stick it in your coat. Along about one o'clock, I'm telling you it goes mighty good. Most people don't know how to cook it right, and it just don't taste good unless it's cooked right. But if it's cooked right, you can eat it for dessert. I just cook it like chicken. I parboil it till it's tender, and then I salt and pepper it up. Bear grease is good too. It's good for anything. Makes the best fish that you ever put in your mouth. Just fluffy and light. You can eat them, too. They still got the flavor to them."

Game did have important uses outside the culinary realm. Indians and early settlers wove hair from the buffalo and possum for clothing. Bird feathers were used to line skins for additional warmth. The English demand for fine deerskin opened up much of the interior of the South.

All the following game recipes come from an open fire method of cooking. In their simplest forms, they are huntsmen's recipes and were prepared out-of-doors. You may try them in your own fireplace or barbecue pit. The difficulty in controlling open fire temperatures makes it impossible to give precise cooking times—a constant watch and your own judgment will be the best guides. Finally, these recipes will lend themselves to substitutions for wild game. Farm rabbit is available, sometimes fresh, frequently frozen, in most markets. You can prepare it in the manner described for the possum. The venison stew can be made with beef. The grilled wild turkey breast—which was a favorite with George Washington—can be answered with its domesticated counterpart. Frozen, if not fresh, quail are shipped all over the country from farms in South Carolina. If they are not available in your market, you might try Cornish game hens.

❧ Possum with Sweet Potatoes ❧

All southerners—black, white, or native—who know game relish possum roasted with sweet potatoes. The two components are inseparable; the dish is practically a cultural symbol of regional pride in the piedmont and mountain areas. Bumper stickers proclaim "Eat More Possum" inland, as they assert "Crayfish Power" in Cajun country.

Horace Kephart first published *Camp Cookery* in 1910. This Shakespeare-quoting wilderness guide provides valuable information for every huntsman and any cook interested in game and open fire preparation. The comparative merits of all types of firewood are delineated; instruction is given for large animal butchering, small fowl and fish preservation—techniques necessary in the wilderness, but worthy in a modern kitchen. His rules of good camp cooking are the rules of all good cooking: "The main secrets of good meals in camp are to have a proper fire, good materials, and then to imprison in each dish, at the outset, its natural juice and characteristic flavor."

To call our possum an opossum, outside of a scientific treatise, is an affectation. Possum is his name wherever he is known and hunted, this country over. He is not good until you have freezing weather; nor is he to be served without sweet potatoes, except in desperate extremity. This is how to serve "possum hot."—

Stick him, and hang him up to bleed until morning. A tub is half filled with hot water (not quite scalding) into which drop the possum and hold him by the tail until the hair will strip. Take him out, lay him on a plank, and pull the hair out with your fingers. Draw, clean, and hang him up to freeze for two or three nights. Then place him in a 5-gallon kettle of cold water, into which throw two pods of red pepper. Parboil for one hour in this pepper-water, which is then thrown out and the kettle refilled with fresh water, wherein he is boiled one hour.

While this is going on, slice and steam some sweet potatoes. Take the possum out, place him in a large Dutch oven, sprinkle him with black pepper, salt, and a pinch or two of sage. A dash of lemon will do no harm. Pack sweet potatoes around him. Pour a pint of water into the oven, put the lid on, and see that it fits tightly. Bake slowly until brown and crisp. Serve hot, *without* gravy. . . .

It is said that possum is not hard to digest even when eaten cold, but the general verdict seems to be that none is ever left over to get cold.

When you have no oven, roast the possum before a high bed of coals, having suspended him by a wet string, which is twisted and untwisted to give a rotary motion, and constantly baste it with a sauce made from red pepper, salt, and vinegar.

Possum may also be baked in clay, with his hide on. Stuff with stale bread and sage, plaster over him with an inch of stiff clay, and bake as previously directed. He will be done in about an hour. (Horace Kephart, *Camp Cookery*)

 *Venison Stew*

A strong French influence marks this cold weather dish of the Huguenot community. Anchovies were prepared in all the better kitchens of coastal settlements and were widely used to season sauces and gravies to add a final fillip, as in this stew.

Yields 6 to 8 servings

1 bottle (750 ml) Cabernet Sauvignon, or any good, dry, red wine
2 cups (475 ml) beef stock
2 bay leaves
1½ teaspoons dried thyme
¼ teaspoon dried red pepper flakes
Zest of one orange removed in strips
2 whole cloves
1½ ounces (43 g) pork sidemeat cut into 1½ inch (3¾ cm) strips
4 pounds (1800 g) lean, boneless venison cut into cubes 1½ inches (3¾ cm) on a side

4 tablespoons (60 g) bacon fat or lard
3 cups (710 ml) sliced onions
1 tablespoon sugar
6 tablespoons flour
1 pound (450 g) canned Italian tomatoes, chopped, with juice
6 anchovies
2 garlic cloves
2 tablespoons chopped, fresh parsley
Salt and freshly ground black pepper

Recommended equipment: A 4-quart (4 L) heavy-bottomed saucepan, Dutch oven.

In the saucepan, bring the wine, stock, bay, thyme, red pepper flakes, orange zest, and cloves to a rapid boil. Reduce to 4 cups (950 ml). Strain and reserve.

Cut strips from the sidemeat, one for each piece of venison. Make a small incision in the center of each piece of venison and insert the larding of sidemeat into it.

Preheat oven to 325°F (163°C).

Heat the fat in the bottom of the Dutch oven over high heat and brown the venison well on all sides. Remove the meat and reserve. Add the onions and sauté with the sugar until lightly browned. Add the flour and cook, stirring, for 3 minutes. Slowly add the wine and stock, stirring all the while. Add tomatoes, return the venison to the pot, and bring to the boil. Cover and place in the preheated oven. Cook very slowly for 3 hours. Remove lid and skim any fat or impurities from the surface. Mash the anchovies and garlic together into a paste. Stir into the stew, re-cover, and cook for 30 more minutes or until venison is tender. Season with the parsley, and salt and pepper to taste. Serve with rice.

❧ Grilled Stuffed Quail ❧

The flavorful stuffing and wood grilling puts a little of the taste of the wild back into farm-raised quail. My favorite accompaniment for this recipe is the Sweet Potato and Pear Soufflé (see page 65).

Yields 4 servings

8 quail, cleaned and split down the backbone (approximately 2 ounces or 60 g each)	2½ tablespoons stale white bread crumbs
4 tablespoons chopped pork sidemeat	2 tablespoons finely chopped carrot
2 large garlic cloves	2 tablespoons finely chopped celery
2 tablespoons mixed green herbs such as parsley, sage, thyme, or parsley alone	Freshly ground black pepper
	1 tablespoon (15 g) bacon fat

Recommended equipment: A charcoal grill.

Note: Build and light charcoal fire approximately 45 minutes before cooking is to begin.

Wash, drain, and dry the quail. Set aside. Chop the pork sidemeat with the garlic and herbs into a fine paste. Add the bread crumbs, carrot, celery, and black pepper, mixing thoroughly.

Stuff the quail, trying not to tear the skin (don't panic if you do). Gently separate the skin from the breast and work the stuffing in between the two. Pack extra stuffing between the thigh and the breast and into any other cavities, using all the stuffing.

Brush the birds with a little of the melted bacon fat and grill over hot coals until golden brown and crisp (or cook under a hot broiler about 4 minutes on each side).

∽ Wild Turkey Steaks with Winter Vegetables ∽

George Washington particularly favored grilled wild turkey while surveying in the wilderness of Virginia in the eighteenth century. The domesticated descendant develops richly and complexly in cooking with both native and introduced winter vegetables.

Yields 4 servings

4 steaks cut from the turkey breast, ⅝ inch (1½ cm) thick, weighing 6 to 8 ounces (170 to 225 g)
1 garlic clove, halved
Juice of one lemon
½ teaspoon salt
½ teaspoon freshly ground black pepper
1 teaspoon dried sage leaves, pulverized
¼ cup (60 ml) peanut oil
6 cups (1400 ml) water
1½ teaspoons salt
8 white onions, weighing a total of 12 ounces (340 g)

3 medium carrots, peeled, quartered, and cut into 1½ inch (3¾ cm) lengths
8 ounces (225 g) turnips, peeled and cut into 24 wedges
8 ounces (225 g) Jerusalem artichokes, peeled and cut into pieces the size of large olives
1 pound (450 g) boiling potatoes, peeled
4 large garlic cloves, peeled
6 slices bacon, chopped
½ teaspoon salt
½ teaspoon freshly ground black pepper
¾ teaspoon dried thyme
¼ cup (60 ml) chopped, fresh parsley

Recommended equipment: A charcoal grill, hickory chips, 5-quart (5 L) saucepan, 10-inch (25 cm) cast-iron skillet or enameled cast-iron sauté pan with lid.

Note: Build and light charcoal fire approximately 45 minutes before cooking is to begin.

Rub the turkey steaks all over with the cut garlic clove. Sprinkle with lemon juice, salt, pepper, and sage. Pour the oil over all and marinate for 2 to 4 hours.

Bring the water to boil in the saucepan and add 1½ teaspoons salt. Blanch the vegetables separately: onions for 5 minutes; carrots, turnips, Jerusalem artichokes for 3 minutes each; the potatoes for 7 minutes; and the garlic for 1 minute. Drain all and let cool.

One and a quarter hours before serving, build a charcoal fire and let it burn down to a good bed of coals. This will take about 45 minutes. During this time soak the hickory chips in water for at least 30 minutes. One-half hour before serving, render the bacon in the skillet or sauté pan over medium low heat until just crisp. Remove, drain, and reserve. Cut the potatoes into ⅓-inch (¾ cm) slices and layer in the bottom of the pan over medium heat. Add the rest of the blanched vegetables, the salt, pepper, thyme, and one-half of the reserved bacon. Cover and cook for 20 minutes, shaking the pan frequently to prevent sticking.

Twenty minutes before serving, add the chips to the coals and grill the steaks, about 4 to 5 minutes on each side. They should brown lightly; guard against overcooking. Transfer the steaks to the skillet, placing them lightly over the vegetables. Sprinkle the rest of the bacon over the steaks, replace the cover and steam gently for 5 to 7 more minutes. Add the chopped fresh parsley and serve immediately.

⟋ *Grilled Rabbit with Chestnut Spoon Bread* ⟍

Such a rich entrée should be served alone as part of a complex meal. A rather rustic and charming touch can be added to this dish by bringing the skillet to the table for serving. Fresh asparagus in lemon butter could precede it nicely, and a simple watercress salad could follow.

Yields 4 to 6 servings

1 rabbit, weighing about 2½ pounds (1125 g), cut into 6 pieces: 2 forelegs with shoulders, 2 loin sections with kidneys, and 2 hind legs

3 slices bacon
2 large garlic cloves
1 teaspoon dried thyme
1 teaspoon dried sage
3 tablespoons vinegar

1 teaspoon salt

1 teaspoon freshly ground black pepper

¼ cup (60 ml) peanut oil

½ cup (118 ml) peeled, chopped, fresh chestnuts (or vacuum packed in a jar)

1 cup (235 ml) yellow cornmeal

1½ teaspoons sugar

½ teaspoon salt

1 cup (235 ml) boiling water

2 eggs, separated

1 cup (235 ml) buttermilk

1 cup (235 ml) grated Cheddar cheese

1 teaspoon baking soda

4 tablespoons (60 g) butter

Recommended equipment: A charcoal grill, hickory chips, food processor or blender, 10-inch (25 cm) cast-iron skillet or enameled cast-iron sauté pan, electric mixer, rubber spatula.

Note: Build and light charcoal fire approximately 45 minutes before cooking is to begin.

Chop the bacon into a paste with the garlic, thyme, and sage. Make small incisions between the muscles of the rabbit pieces and pack the seasonings into them. Rub each piece well with vinegar, salt, and pepper, and marinate in the oil, turning occasionally, for 4 to 6 hours.

Preheat oven to 325°F (163°C).

While the rabbit is marinating, put the fresh or vacuum-packed chestnuts in the preheated oven for 10 to 12 minutes, or until lightly dried. Remove, let cool, and pulverize in a blender or food processor until fine as cornmeal. Reserve.

Build a good fire in the grill and let the flames die down to a hot bed of coals. During this time soak the hickory chips in water for at least 30 minutes. Drain the chips and add to the fire. Place the rabbit on the grill and brown well on all sides, about 15 to 20 minutes total cooking time. Watch carefully and do not let the meat overcook.

Preheat oven to 375°F (190°C).

Combine the chestnut flour, cornmeal, sugar, and salt in a bowl. Pour the boiling water over, stir well and let sit for 10 minutes. Separate the eggs and reserve the whites. Beat the yolks with the buttermilk and stir into the batter. Add the cheese and soda. Beat the egg whites until stiff and fold in. Melt the butter in the skillet or sauté pan over medium heat. Pour the batter into the skillet all at once. Arrange the rabbit pieces over the top of the batter and put into the preheated oven immediately.

Reduce heat to 325°F (163°C). Bake 40 minutes or until spoon bread has risen, is set, and is lightly browned. Serve immediately.

Salads, Pickles, and Condiments

So I merely slammed the door behind me and went down and made some green-tomato pickle. Somebody had to do it.

Eudora Welty, "Why I Live at the P.O."

Wilted Salads

Throughout the hill and mountain regions of the South, wilted salad is a favorite. It was an ingenious solution to the general lack of vegetable or olive oil in the region (in and around Charleston the African-introduced benne or sesame seed was pressed, but the use of the oil was never widespread). The bacon fat used as the base of the dressing must be hot since it congeals at room temperature. It delightfully wilts—but does not cook—the fresh, raw lettuce. Traditionally, southerners often wilted wild greens gathered when young—chickweed, dandelions, purslane, sorrel, land cress (creasie greens), watercress, corn lettuce (or mâche). Any tender lettuces will work: Boston, Bibb, leaf, and so forth. Very thinly sliced cucumbers are delicious served in this manner. Whatever you serve, your preparations must be well thought out, all ingredients premeasured, and at hand. Then clear a path to the table before you begin; the salad must be rushed to the diners!

Yields 4 servings

4 cups (1 L) water
1 or 2 eggs at room temperature
1 large head Boston lettuce or 12 ounces (340 g) mixed greens
6 slices bacon, coarsely chopped

1 to 2 tablespoons peanut oil (optional)
²/₃ cup (160 ml) thinly sliced scallions
3 to 4 tablespoons vinegar

¹/₂ teaspoon sugar
¹/₂ teaspoon salt
Freshly ground black pepper to
    taste

Recommended equipment: A 1¹/₂-quart (1¹/₂ L) saucepan, 10-inch (25 cm) cast-iron skillet or enameled cast-iron sauté pan.

In the saucepan, bring the water to a boil and place the egg(s) in it to cook 5 minutes. Remove and let cool. Shell and chop roughly when ready to serve.

Wash the lettuce or greens carefully, drain, and place between layers of paper towels to dry. Most salads are disappointing when executed with wet greens; this one especially so. Chill the leaves; when ready to serve, tear them into large bite-sized pieces.

Render the bacon slowly in the skillet or sauté pan over low to medium heat. Remove bacon when just crisp and reserve the fat in the pan.

At this point be prepared to work quickly—be sure greens are out, torn, and ready for tossing. Have all other ingredients pre-measured and add the peanut oil to the pan if needed. Raise heat to high and sauté the scallions very quickly, about 90 seconds. Add the vinegar to the pan along with the sugar and salt, and boil hard for 1 minute. Pour the bubbling sauce over the torn greens and toss quickly. Season well with black pepper. Garnish with the reserved bacon and chopped egg. Serve immediately.

☙ Boiled Dressing ❧

Had the English settlers established the olive tree, as they tried, on North Carolina's Outer Banks, the story of salad in the South would have been a lot different. Since the region had essentially no vegetable oils before the late nineteenth century, vinaigrettes and mayonnaises were confined to the tables of the very rich who could afford imported olive oil. Boiled dressing was the ingenious solution for the rest of the people. (Mayonnaise was once so exotic that Eudora Welty wrote of its coming to Jackson, Mississippi.) The ability of an egg yolk to absorb fat, as in mayonnaise, is still recognized, but now butter and cream make the sauce unctuous. The astute cook will notice that boiled dressing is, in fact, a member of the hollandaise family, and that it actually is not boiled. This sauce has traditionally bound the many composed salads of the South: cabbage, potato, bean, chicken—the list is as long as the grocery list.

Yields approximately 1½ cups

1 teaspoon dry mustard	½ cup (118 ml) cold water
2 teaspoons sugar	2 egg yolks, beaten
½ teaspoon salt	3 tablespoons apple cider vinegar
2 tablespoons flour	3 tablespoons (45 g) butter
⅛ teaspoon white pepper	3 tablespoons heavy cream

Recommended equipment: A double boiler, wire whisk.

Sift the dry ingredients into the top of the double boiler. Stirring slowly and constantly with the whisk, add the cold water in a steady stream until smoothly combined. Add the egg yolks and vinegar and place over boiling water in the bottom of the double boiler. Stir constantly and watch carefully—it will thicken in the blink of an eye. Take the mixture off the heat and beat in the butter. Then slowly beat in the cream. Refrigerate.

Creole Potato Salad

Yields 4 to 6 servings

1¾ pounds (800 g) new potatoes, white or red	½ teaspoon freshly ground black pepper
1 tablespoon salt	½ cup (118 ml) chopped green bell pepper
6 quarts (6 L) water	½ cup (118 ml) chopped celery
1 cup (235 ml) Boiled Dressing (see page 134)	⅔ cup (160 ml) chopped scallions
2 tablespoons Creole Mustard (see page 137)	1 tablespoon chopped fresh basil
1½ teaspoons salt	1 tablespoon chopped fresh parsley

Recommended equipment: An 8-quart (8 L) stockpot, large stainless steel or glass bowl.

Bring water and salt to a boil in the stockpot and add potatoes in their jackets. Boil until tender, approximately 20 minutes depending on size. Drain and rinse. Slice into ¼ inch (½ cm) slices while still hot and toss very gently with the Boiled Dressing, Creole Mustard, salt, and pepper. Chill until serving time. Just before serving, gently fold in the chopped vegetables and herbs.

⚬ Coleslaw ⚬

The recipe which follows can be made the year round. In the summer the garden offers many opportunities: fresh peas, carrots for grating, radishes to be thinly sliced, tomatoes, green peppers, and fresh dill or basil. The cabbage should remain the essential feature of the salad; don't overwhelm it with competing ingredients which should be present as complements. Other than this simple reminder, the only rule for coleslaw is that it reflect the season.

Yields 4 servings

Basic recipe

4 cups (950 ml) shredded, raw
   cabbage
9 to 10 tablespoons Boiled
   Dressing (see page 134)

$1/4$ cup (60 ml) chopped scallions
   or red onion
$1/4$ teaspoon salt
Freshly ground black pepper to
   taste (generous quantity)

Combine above ingredients, cover, and chill one hour before serving.
    The basic recipe is a background against which many seasonal variations are played. In the winter I might add one or all of the following seasonings:

$1/16$ teaspoon whole celery seed
1 teaspoon Creole Mustard (see
   page 137)
2 to 4 tablespoons chopped,
   fresh parsley or chervil

~ Creole Mustard ~

Zatarain's has supplied generations of Louisiana cooks with a fine line of traditional seasonings, from shrimp boil to filé, the powdered sassafras leaf used to thicken gumbo. Their mustard is held in esteem and sets a standard in New Orleans. If it is unavailable in your area, here is another, hotter version, pebbly with cracked whole seeds, and much in the Creole style. Prepared mustard loses its piquancy quickly; if your mustard needs aren't great, you can prepare half of the given amount. Use it as a condiment the way you use other mustards—in salads, with cold meats and seafoods, and so forth. In cooking, coat joints of meat before roasting and add it to sauces and gravies.

Yields a generous ½ cup

¼ cup (60 ml) white wine vinegar
2 tablespoons water
2 tablespoons vegetable oil
⅛ teaspoon celery seed
¹⁄₁₆ teaspoon ground white pepper
2 whole cloves

1 garlic clove, sliced
½ teaspoon salt
½ teaspoon sugar
4 tablespoons whole mustard seed
2 tablespoons ground mustard

Recommended equipment: A small saucepan with lid, blender or food processor.

Combine the vinegar, water, oil, celery seed, white pepper, cloves, garlic, salt, and sugar in the saucepan. Cover tightly and bring to a rapid boil over high heat. When the boiling point is reached, remove the pan from the burner and let sit, covered, for 30 minutes to steep. Strain the liquid and discard the solids. Put the whole mustard seed and the ground seed into the container of a blender or food processor, activating the blades for approximately 1 minute. Then slowly pour in the liquid and process as long as desired. Creole-style mustard is usually pebbly, with cracked seeds discernible. This also may be made by first using a mortar and pestle to crack the seeds well and then whisking in the liquid.

~ Southern Style Mayonnaise ~

When mayonnaise was made in the South, it took on a distinctly southern flavor, slightly sweet from sugar, hot from cayenne, and fruity from the region's apple cider vinegar. Paprika, which is so popular in the South, gives it a slightly rosy tinge. Alone, mayonnaise tops the summer's rich ripe tomatoes or, with a grating of sharp cheddar cheese, converts poached pears into a first salad course. This regional mayonnaise is the base of other cold sauces such as tartar, which is served with hot fried foods, or remoulade, which accompanies cold seafood.

Yields 3 cups

4 large egg yolks
1/4 cup (60 ml) apple cider vinegar
1 teaspoon salt
1/4 teaspoon dry mustard
1/4 teaspoon paprika

Pinch sugar
1/4 teaspoon white pepper
2 1/2 cups (590 ml) peanut oil or
    light olive oil

Recommended equipment: A blender or food processor.

Beat the egg yolks and vinegar with a fork in a small bowl. Mix the dry ingredients well to avoid lumping and stir into the egg yolks. In the blender or processor, beat the egg yolk mixture, and very slowly, drop by drop at first, begin to add the oil. Once the yolks have absorbed a tablespoon or so of oil, add the oil in a steady but thin stream. Stop occasionally and scrape down the sides. Store in the refrigerator. Keeps a week or so.

~ Tartar Sauce ~

Yields about 2 1/2 cups

1 1/2 cups (350 ml) Southern Style
    Mayonnaise (see page 138)
1/3 cup (80 ml) sweet pickle relish
1/4 cup (60 ml) minced onion
1/4 cup (60 ml) minced celery

2 teaspoons fresh, chopped
    tarragon
1 tablespoon fresh, chopped
    parsley
8 drops Tabasco sauce

Optional: Worcestershire sauce, lemon juice to taste

Combine all the ingredients and stir well. Chill for at least 30 minutes before serving to develop flavor.

❧ Shrimp Remoulade ❧

One of the great pleasures of New Orleans is sampling the same traditional dish in different restaurants. We used to go back and forth from Antoine's to Galatoire's comparing the legendary Oysters Rockefeller, arguing up and down the steamy street, and taking a refresher course at the Acme Oyster Bar on what the au naturel bivalve was all about. Shrimp remoulades were equally debated, but I would have to vote the best I ever tasted was the first, at Arnaud's; it was hotter than any cold food I could have imagined.

Yields 4 servings

1 pound (454 g) cold, peeled, cooked shrimp (see page 85)

1¼ cups (300 ml) Southern Style Mayonnaise (see page 138)

4 tablespoons Creole Mustard (see page 137) or a strong Dijon-style mustard

5 tablespoons minced scallions

3 tablespoons fresh, chopped parsley

1 to 2 tablespoons grated horseradish

4 to 6 anchovy fillets, rinsed and chopped

1 tablespoon capers, chopped

½ teaspoon white pepper, or more to taste

Lemon juice, Tabasco sauce to taste

Lettuce leaves or watercress

Prepare the shrimp and refrigerate. Combine mayonnaise and all the seasonings, cover and chill for at least 30 minutes.

Fifteen minutes before serving, combine sauce and shrimp and return to the refrigerator. Serve atop lettuce leaves or watercress on chilled plates.

❧ Deviled Eggs ❧

"You can't have too many deviled eggs" was a maxim for entertaining in my mother's kitchen, and it's never been disproved in my experience. Deviled eggs are perfect for parties, especially when children are present. Mine, at least, will pass up all sorts of sweets and other less nutritious treats for a deviled egg. Any number of variations—fillings of shrimp, country ham, chutney—is possible, but a good dose of mustard is required. Deviled comes from the French *à diable,* which in cooking always means mustard.

Yields 12 pieces

6 eggs at room temperature
3 cups (700 ml) water
¼ cup (60 ml) Southern Style
   Mayonnaise (see page 138)

2 tablespoons mustard, Dijon-
   style, American-style, or
   Creole (see page 137)
3 teaspoons pickle relish
Salt and white pepper to taste

Recommended equipment: A 1½-quart (1½ L) saucepan, colander.

Bring the water to a rapid boil and carefully add the eggs. Cook for 11 minutes, drain, cool, then refrigerate.

When cold, peel the eggs, cut in half lengthwise, and remove the yolks. Beat the yolks with the mayonnaise, mustard, and pickle relish. Season to taste with salt and pepper. Fill the cavity of the whites with the deviled mixture, cover, and refrigerate. Garnish as desired just before serving—with paprika, a dab of relish, chopped olives, sliced scallions, whatever.

◖ Tomato Aspic ◗

The charm of some of our best dishes in the South is lost in repetition or forgotten in a search for novelty. A few years ago in France, after eating meal after meal with the then ubiquitous vegetable terrine course, I found myself longing for the simple and direct pleasure of the tomato aspics of the South. American cooks often disregard these aspics, preferring such foreign dishes as gazpacho, but a fresh tomato aspic is just such a chunky garden set up by gelatin. In the winter, an aspic may be perfectly plain, but in the summer whatever comes from the garden goes into it—bell peppers, cucumbers, and so on. Tomato aspics are usually served as a salad course before a roast, on lettuce with homemade mayonnaise. For special occasions, artichoke hearts, crabmeat, shrimp or poached fish are added for a more substantial course.

1 28-ounce (340 g) can tomatoes	2 tablespoons minced scallions
2 sprigs fresh tarragon	3 tablespoons minced celery
2 sprigs fresh thyme	1 tablespoon fresh, chopped
Pinch red pepper flakes	herbs—parsley, chives, basil
2 envelopes gelatin	Tabasco sauce
¹⁄₄ cup (60 ml) cold water	

Recommended equipment: A food processor or blender, small saucepan, strainer.

Purée the tomatoes and put in saucepan with the tarragon, thyme, and pepper. Bring to a boil and simmer 20 minutes. Strain well, pressing the residue to release all juices.

Soften the gelatin in the cold water. Stir into the warm juice until dissolved. Set over a bowl of ice water, and stir occasionally until the aspic begins to thicken. Add scallions, celery, and herbs and taste for salt, pepper, and Tabasco.

Pour into a lightly oiled mold or individual ramekins. Chill well, at least 3 hours. Turn out onto lettuce and garnish with Southern Style Mayonnaise.

☙ Cucumbers and Onions ❧

This dish has no name other than cucumbers and onions. Though it is a great summer favorite throughout the South, and one of the region's true native salads, by its nature it is most likely a stand-in for the pickles put up the previous summer and consumed during the winter. Come July, last year's crop is gone and this year's crop has some time to go on the shelf before maturity. There is more than a little charm in this refreshing combination, and, with its lower salt content, can be consumed much more heartily than its vintage cousin, the bread-and-butter pickle. Often, it is prepared without sugar, salt, or many of the flavorings below.

Yields 8 to 10 servings

4 cups (950 ml) sliced cucumbers	2 cups (475 ml) apple cider
2 teaspoons salt	vinegar
4 cups (950 ml) sliced onions	6 teaspoons sugar

2 sprigs fresh thyme	3 tablespoons peanut or olive oil
1 garlic clove	⅓ cup (80 ml) chopped, fresh
1 red pepper pod	parsley

Recommended equipment: A colander, 4-quart (4 L) stainless steel or glass bowl.

Toss the thinly sliced cucumbers with the salt and let drain in a colander for 15 minutes. Then submerge in ice water and soak for 5 minutes more. Drain well and place in a stainless steel or glass bowl with the onions.

Boil the vinegar and sugar with the rest of the ingredients, except for the parsley. Pour hot over the vegetables, toss, cover, and refrigerate. Serve when very cold, adding the chopped parsley just before the dish goes to the table.

Pickles

Pickles and relishes are a staple of every southern pantry. They are made from every imaginable garden product including the exotic: green tomatoes, walnuts, watermelons, mangoes, pumpkins, radishes, peaches, palm hearts. All these forceful flavors provide variety and excitement when a meal may be otherwise dull. In former days, they were of special interest in winter when a staple diet of preserved pork, dried beans, and corn bread became monotonous. Relishes are rarely used in cooking, but occasionally a spoonful of this or that is stirred into a sauce or gravy. More frequently, a little of these sweet and sour condiments is added to cold dishes and salads such as stuffed eggs or potato salad. Most often, they are served separately, a spoonful added at the table to black-eyed peas or over country ham.

Pickled Peaches

A pickled peach was the favorite relish of all the children in my family. Such a challenge to keep it on the plate—the slightest false move would set it skittering over the rim and across the table, but how we loved its sweet and sour tang! This was a special treat for Sunday afternoon dinners or holiday meals, and especially good with a salty ham or a sage-infused roast hen.

Salads

Yields 4 quarts

3 pounds (1350 g) sugar
3 cups (710 ml) white vinegar
2 sticks of cinnamon, halved
1½ tablespoons whole cloves

¼ teaspoon red pepper flakes
¼ teaspoon white pepper
¼ teaspoon mustard seed, whole
36 perfect small peaches

Recommended equipment: An open kettle canner, four 1-quart (1 L) glass jars with rings and lids for vacuum seal, rubber-tipped tongs.

Sterilize the jars, their lids and rings, by boiling over high heat for 10 minutes. Remove with tongs, drain, and let air dry in oven at 250°F (121°C).

Blanch the peaches in boiling water for 45 seconds. Plunge into cold water bath and peel as soon as the fruit is cool enough to handle. Set aside.

Prepare the pickling solution by combining sugar, vinegar, and all the spices. Boil for 10 minutes. Drop the peeled peaches into the spiced broth and poach for 5 minutes at the barest simmer.

Pack 9 peaches into each of the hot jars and pour the boiling broth over the peaches to a level ½ inch (1 cm) below the top of the jar. Clean the rim and threads with a sterile cloth. Top with a lid and ring. With the tongs, lower the jars into the boiling water of the kettle canner and boil hard for 10 minutes. Remove the jars and let cool. Store in a cool, dark place for 6 weeks before serving.

Pickled Okra

I am a great fan of okra in any form, and though I would lobby any theater to serve fried okra in place of popcorn, perhaps pickled okra is most palatable to the uninitiated. A simple southern hors d'oeuvre platter might be made of pickled okra with deviled eggs, green onions, celery, radishes, and pimento cheese. The okra has never failed to win converts and gives guests freedom to use one of the favorite lines of cocktail party chitchat, "I remember the first time I ever tasted . . ."

2¹/₂ pounds (1125 g) very small okra pods

6 garlic cloves, peeled

6 heads of dill weed

12 dried red pepper pods

3 teaspoons mustard seeds

48 black peppercorns

5¹/₃ cups (1250 ml) white vinegar

3³/₄ cups (890 ml) water

3 tablespoons pickling salt

Recommended equipment: An open kettle canner, 4-quart (4 L) stainless steel or enamel saucepan, six 1-pint (500 ml) glass jars with lids and rings for vacuum seal, rubber-tipped tongs.

Sterilize the jars, their lids, and rings by boiling over high heat for 10 minutes. When the jars are sterile, remove them with tongs, drain, and let air dry.

Meanwhile, wash the okra well in cold water, trim the stems, but do not remove the cap, which is quite tasty and crisp in the finished product. Pack the okra in the dry bottles, alternating the blossom and stem ends. Divide the garlic, dill, pepper pods, mustard seeds, and peppercorns evenly among the 6 jars.

In the saucepan, combine the vinegar, water, and salt and bring to a boil over high heat. Pour the boiling brine over the okra to a level ¹/₂ inch (1 cm) below the top of the jar. Top with a lid and ring. With the tongs, lower the jars into the boiling water of a kettle canner and boil hard for 5 minutes. Remove the jars and let cool. Store for 6 to 8 weeks in a cool, dark place before using.

Variations: Use thyme or tarragon sprigs instead of (but not in addition to) dill weed.

⟨ Pickled Oysters ⟩

At an oyster supper, it is usual to have all the various preparations of oysters, fried, stewed, broiled, roasted, raw, and in patties.

Maryland's Way

This Lucullan Chesapeake oyster supper would seem complete but for one recipe prepared throughout the southern coastlands—pickled oysters. A usually temporary solution to a surfeit of bivalves, the oysters are actually marinated rather than pickled and are served as hors d'oeuvres, salads, or part of a cold buffet. Do not prepare the onion garnish ahead of time; the onions will be more strongly flavored than if chopped just before serving time and will overpower the oysters.

Yields 6 servings

1 quart (1 L) shucked oysters	1/2 teaspoon red pepper flakes
24 whole black peppercorns	1/2 teaspoon salt
2 whole cloves	1 cup (235 ml) cold water
4 whole allspice	1/4 cup (60 ml) dry white wine
1 teaspoon whole mustard seeds	1/4 cup (60 ml) vinegar

To serve

1 cup (235 ml) chopped red onion
2 tablespoons chopped, fresh
 parsley
2 teaspoons lemon juice
1/4 cup (60 ml) vegetable oil

Recommended equipment: A mortar and pestle, 1½-quart (1½ L) saucepan, slotted spoon.

Drain the oysters and reserve the liquid. Pound the spices: peppercorns, cloves, allspice, mustard seeds, and red pepper flakes in a mortar and pestle until well cracked, but not finely ground. Combine with salt and add to water, wine, vinegar, and reserved liquor from the oysters. Bring rapidly to a boil, reduce heat, and simmer for 15 minutes. Add the oysters and cook until the edges curl and the bodies plump—about 3 minutes. Remove with a slotted spoon and chill. Reduce the liquid to 1 cup (235 ml) and pour over the oysters. Cover and refrigerate overnight.

To serve, drain off and discard the liquid from the oysters. Mix the chopped onion, parsley, lemon juice, and oil and toss with the oysters. Serve very cold with crackers as an hors d'oeuvre, or with tomatoes, hard-boiled eggs, and Boston lettuce as a salad.

One of my most distinct early food memories is also one of my most unhappy. In my mind I can re-create the emanation of a pot of field peas simmering with a ham hock. As soon as a bowl was filled with them for the dinner table, my grandmother began shaving the tiniest slivers of a green cayenne pepper directly onto the peas. My curiosity led me too close, and just as I peered over the table top and into those peas—pow!—the cayenne caught me right in the eye. I lost that battle, but won the war, holding my own, though tearfully, in Mexico years later.

Cayenne pods, both green and red, fresh and dried, are the universal seasoning agents of southern cooking. Every pot of greens or peas—almost every vegetable cooked in the South—will be paired with a pepper pod sooner or later. In one of its most unusual appearances, and true to the commonplace that a southerner will make a jelly out of anything, cayenne stars as a jelly. Delicious with cold meats, especially country hams and smoked fowl, it is a hot and sour and sweet condiment in the Hunam-Chinese vein and much more complex than the ubiquitous mint jelly. A staple of southern cocktail parties, it is served with cream cheese and crackers. Now, with the renaissance of local cheese making, I offer it with fresh goat cheese from our farmers' market.

Yields 3½ pints

1½ cups (355 ml) white or apple-cider vinegar

6 cups (1209 g) sugar

½ cup (118 ml) chopped hot peppers, seeds removed

1 cup (235 ml) chopped green bell peppers, seeds removed

6 to 8 ounces (170 to 225 g) liquid pectin, depending on the brand—check the process description before purchasing

⅔ cup (160 ml) chopped scallions

¼ cup (60 ml) shredded, fresh basil

Recommended equipment: An 8-quart (8 L) stockpot for sterilizing the jars, rubber-tipped tongs, 4-quart (4 L) stainless steel or enamel saucepan, seven ½-pint (250 ml) glass jars with rings and lids for vacuum seal.

Sterilize the jars, their lids, and rings by boiling over high heat for 10 minutes. When jars are sterile, remove with tongs, drain, and let air dry.

Salads

Bring the vinegar and sugar to the boil in the saucepan and cook 5 minutes. Add both the hot and sweet peppers and boil an additional minute. Then add liquid pectin, scallions, and basil. Boil rapidly for 1 more minute. Pour into dry jars. Clean jar rims and threads with a clean towel dipped into boiling water. Secure tops. Invert 20 seconds to seal, then turn upright to cool. As with any jelly, this is ready to eat now. Store the rest in a cool, dark place.

∽ *Pepper Sauce* ∾

Pepper sauce is usually reserved for table use, flavoring cooked vegetables, especially greens, but I often use it in salad dressings, and so forth, in short, any place where vinegar may be called for.

Yields 1 pint

8 to 10 green cayenne peppers
10 ounces (295 ml) white or apple
   cider vinegar

Recommended equipment: A one-pint (500 ml) glass jar, 1¹/₂-quart (1¹/₂ L) stainless steel saucepan (for method 2).

Method 1: Pack the peppers into the clean jar. Pour the cold vinegar over and cover tightly. Set aside for 10 days in a cool, dark place.

Method 2: Pack the peppers into the clean jar. Bring the vinegar to a boil in the saucepan. Immediately pour over the peppers. Let cool; cover tightly. Set aside for 7 days.

Do not process in a canner or by a canning process in either method.

∽ *Cajun Tomato Sauce* ∾

This fresh piquant sauce is an example of what southerners call a "table sauce," a condiment served cold or at room temperature and added to hot foods at the table. It is excellent with the Rice Omelet, Natchitoches Meat Pies, Field Peas, and Fried Vegetables (see pages 45, 110, 66–67, and 58).

1 cup (235 ml) chopped, fresh tomato (1 large tomato—do not peel or seed)

½ cup (118 ml) scallions, sliced

1 teaspoon or more minced, fresh, green cayenne pepper, seeds removed

¼ cup (60 ml) chopped fresh parsley

¼ teaspoon salt

½ teaspoon sugar

2 tablespoons peanut oil

1 tablespoon Pepper Sauce (see page 147) or vinegar

Combine all ingredients 15 minutes before serving.

‿◞ Green Tomato Relish ◟‿

Southern cold buffets are still elaborate affairs, featuring hams, smoked turkeys, corned beef, and all types of seafood. Green tomato relish would be one of many cold condiments to accompany the meats.

Yields 4 pints

4 quarts (3¾ L) sliced green tomatoes (unpeeled)

1 tablespoon pickling salt

6 cups (1400 ml) thinly sliced onions

2 tablespoons ground mustard

1 tablespoon white pepper

1 tablespoon ground ginger

1 tablespoon ground allspice

1 teaspoon dried red pepper flakes

12 ounces (340 g) light brown sugar

2½ cups (590 ml) white vinegar

Recommended equipment: A 3-quart (3 L) heavy-bottomed saucepan, stoneware crock, four 1-pint (500 ml) glass jars with rings and lids for vacuum seal, open kettle canner, rubber-tipped tongs.

Put the sliced tomatoes in the stoneware crock, sprinkling each layer with salt. Let stand overnight and drain off the juice. Chop the tomatoes roughly. Add to the heavy-bottomed saucepan along with the onions, mustard, pepper, ginger, allspice, red pepper flakes, and brown sugar. Pour the vinegar over all, bring to a simmer and cook very gently for 1½ hours.

Sterilize the jars, their lids, and rings by boiling for 10 minutes. Dry the jars by draining them. Do not use a cloth to dry. While the jars are hot, pack the relish in them and cover with lids and rings. Process

10 minutes in boiling water in an open kettle canner. Store about 4 weeks in a cool, dark place before using.

❧ Mushroom Catsup ☙

A catsup in the eighteenth and nineteenth centuries was a source of piquancy for many dishes, a far more diverse seasoning than what passes under that name today. The word comes from an oriental term for the brine of pickled fish or shellfish; the *Oxford English Dictionary* defines it as "almost any salty extract of fish, shellfish, fruits, vegetables, or mushrooms." The ubiquitous tomato sauce we know is not a fair representative of this large family of condiments.

Southern cooks would pickle unripened English or black walnuts for a walnut catsup. The nuts had to be green enough to be pricked through with a pin, and were put into a spiced brine, left to stand, and then strained out. Reduced and bottled, the liquid functioned in cooking much like a Worcestershire sauce. Many old southern recipes have been corrupted in later years by the modern cook's ignorance of such sauces. Knowing only the tomato catsup, cooks have added it erroneously. Frequently, Worcestershire or an oriental oyster sauce would have been closer to the original intention. When you come across southern recipes that call for catsup, try imaginatively to reconstruct them historically. If tomato catsup seems at cross-purposes with the intended development of flavors, omit it.

A well-flavored catsup can be made from commercial mushrooms, but if you have access to chanterelles, flaps, or other foraged wild mushrooms, use them, by themselves or in combination. Shiitake mushrooms, now appearing in many markets, may be employed as well, though their high price will limit their use. Mushroom catsup as a flavoring is added to stews, soups, sauces, and gravies. In older southern cookbooks, this preparation is often referred to as mushroom soy, or simply, soy.

Yields about 1 pint

1½ pounds (675 g) fresh
   mushrooms, thinly sliced
2½ teaspoons pickling salt
2 to 3 ounces (60 to 85 g) dried
   porcini or cèpes

3½ cups (830 ml) water
1 large onion, thinly sliced
4 large garlic cloves, roughly
   chopped
36 black peppercorns

⅛ teaspoon whole celery seed	1½ teaspoons dried thyme
1 bay leaf	1 teaspoon dried basil
¼ teaspoon red pepper flakes	¼ cup (60 ml) vinegar
2 whole cloves	

Recommended equipment: A stoneware crock; two saucepans, one 1½ quart (1½ L) and one 5 quart (5 L); strainer; cheesecloth if desired.

Strew the sliced mushrooms in layers in the stoneware crock, sprinkling each layer with salt. Set aside for 6 hours in a cool, dark place. Later, combine dried mushrooms, water, onion, garlic, black peppercorns, celery seed, bay, red pepper flakes, cloves, thyme, and basil in the smaller saucepan and bring to a full boil. Reduce heat immediately and keep at a bare simmer for 30 minutes. Pour over the salted mushrooms and stir about roughly. Set aside for 6 more hours, stirring to bruise occasionally.

Turn the entire contents of the crock into the larger saucepan, bring to a boil over high heat, and boil hard 10 minutes. Let cool and strain through a colander, firmly pressing the solids to release their juices. Discard the mushroom debris and return the liquid to the smaller saucepan. Add the vinegar at this point and boil hard for 2 minutes. Strain again, through cheesecloth, if desired, or bottle as is. Cool to room temperature. Keeps well under refrigeration.

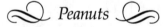

Peanuts

Peanuts are not nuts at all but a member of the bean family, and are known scientifically as *Arachis hypogaea*. The fruit has a curious development: after the flowers are fertilized, they wither to the ground and bury themselves; the seedpods mature subterraneously. Peanuts are usually harvested by uprooting the whole plant to dry the nuts.

Nicknames abound for the peanut; groundnut is often seen in older cookbooks. One common southern name, goober or goober-pea, comes directly from the African "nguba." Though the peanut originated in Brazil, it was from Africa that North America received it as an important culinary item. In Guinea the peanut had quickly become a staple food after its Portuguese introduction. Its food value is great, and it was a common ship food for the enslaved blacks en route to the Americas.

In southern cooking the peanut is used in great variety. Soups are

Salads

made from it, many dressings and stuffings for fowl and game are accented by it, and it garnishes vegetable casseroles. Numerous candies and cookies feature it; the best known is peanut brittle which is often called groundnut cake in the South. Black women known as "maumas" sold the sweets wrapped in paper on the streets of Charleston. The flavor of the peanut is pervasive in almost all of its culinary uses, yet it yields a tasteless oil of the highest quality for frying and sautéing.

ᘛ Hot and Spicy Peanuts ᘚ

Fresh peanuts, simply prepared, are probably the most popular and common between-meal eating of the region. My father would prepare the sautéed peanuts below on cold winter nights, from a crop we had tended together the previous summer.

Yields about 1½ cups

1 teaspoon salt
½ teaspoon paprika
¼ teaspoon (or more) ground
   cayenne
½ teaspoon (or more) sugar

1 tablespoon peanut oil
1½ cups (355 ml) raw, shelled
   peanuts
1½ tablespoons water

Recommended equipment: A 10-inch (25 cm) cast-iron skillet or enameled cast-iron sauté pan.

Combine the salt, paprika, cayenne, and sugar and reserve. Heat the peanut oil in the skillet or sauté pan over medium high heat. Add the raw peanuts (in their skins), shaking the skillet frequently to prevent their scorching. When the peanuts are golden brown throughout (after 8 to 10 minutes), sprinkle the combined dry seasonings over all and shake well. Carefully, but immediately, pour in the water and agitate to help the flavorings coat the peanuts. Serve immediately or let cool. These will keep for weeks in an airtight container.

∽ Boiled Peanuts ∾

Boiled peanuts are surely a strange snack, but were once as popular as roasted ones. I remember well my Great-great-aunt Sara's search for her personal vender among the stalls of the Farmers' Market in Columbia, South Carolina.

Yields 2 cups

2 cups (475 ml) green peanuts,
    raw and in the shell
4 cups (950 ml) water
1½ teaspoons salt

Recommended equipment: A 3-quart (3 L) saucepan, strainer.

Put the peanuts, in their shells, into a saucepan, add the water and salt, and bring to a boil. Reduce the heat to a good simmer and cook approximately 25 minutes. Time will vary depending upon the size and freshness of the peanuts. When done, the kernel should have swollen to fill the pod well and the taste of raw starch will have been dissipated. The peanut will remain slightly chewy. Serve hot still in the shell, or cold after draining.

∽ Roasted Peanuts ∾

No commercial product can ever taste as rich as fresh peanuts roasted at home. I find the brined nuts on the market particularly distasteful, the soaking destroying texture and taste.

Yields 1 pound

1 pound (450 g) peanuts, raw in
    the shell

Preheat oven to 375°F (190°C).
    Put the peanuts on a wide baking sheet and place on the middle shelf of the preheated oven. Shake the pan every 5 minutes to prevent scorching on any one side. Peanuts will be done in 20 minutes or so depending on size and maturity.

Desserts

I didn't fool with any of the barbecue, just ate ham and chicken. And then I had some chicken salad, and Susie wanted me to try some potato salad, so I tried that too, and then we had a good many hot rolls and some stuffed eggs and some pickles and some coconut cake and some chocolate cake. I had been saving myself up for Aunt Rachel's chess pies and put three on my plate when I started out, but by the time I got to them I wasn't really hungry and I let Susie eat one of mine.

Caroline Gordon, "The Petrified Woman"

Mardi Gras Pudding with Caramel Brandy Sauce
(Pouding de Riz au Caramel Renversée)

Rice puddings, despite their devotees, are generally considered plebeian dishes—family delights, perhaps, but not company fare. This version is the exception, haute French in its beautiful caramel coating and flashy with its unexpected bits of exotic glacéed fruits. It expresses well the year-round carnival atmosphere of the two most colorful southern ports, Mobile and New Orleans. Serve it slightly warmer than room temperature, cut into wedges, with whipped cream. One of the two fruit sauces could also accompany it (see recipes). In New Orleans this elegant dessert would be known according to its French name shown above. You may wish to appropriate this appellation to keep your guests in suspense. They will not be disappointed to see this rice pudding.

3½ cups (830 ml) milk
½ cup (118 ml) heavy cream
¾ cup (180 ml) raw long grain rice
¼ cup (50 g) sugar
¼ teaspoon salt
1½ inch (3¾ cm) piece of cinnamon stick

¼ teaspoon freshly grated nutmeg
2 tablespoons finely chopped glacéed fruit
2 tablespoons dried currants
3 eggs
1 tablespoon vanilla extract

For caramelizing the baking dish

¾ cup (151 g) sugar
⅓ cup (80 ml) water
2 tablespoons brandy

For the bain-marie

Boiling water

Recommended equipment: A glass or ceramic soufflé dish and a larger pan for this to sit in for a bain-marie; 10-inch (25 cm) cast-iron skillet or enameled cast-iron sauté pan; 3-quart (3 L) saucepan; medium mixing bowl; aluminum foil.

For the caramel
Heat the sugar and water together in the skillet over medium heat until it reaches a rich honey color. Immediately remove from heat and stir very carefully to cool. Add brandy just as the caramel begins to thicken and pour into the soufflé dish. Rotate the dish quickly, but carefully, to coat the sides well so that the pudding can be easily unmolded.

Combine the milk, cream, rice, sugar, salt, cinnamon stick, and nutmeg in the saucepan and cook gently until rice is very soft. This will take approximately 35 to 40 minutes. Preheat oven to 350°F (177°C).

Remove rice from heat when done and discard cinnamon stick. Add glacéed fruit and currants and cool to lukewarm. Beat the eggs well with the vanilla extract in the mixing bowl and stir into the rice. Pour all of the ingredients into the caramelized dish, cover tightly with aluminum foil, place in the larger baking pan, and add 1 inch (2½ cm)

Desserts

of boiling water for a bain-marie. Bake about 45 minutes or until the pudding is set.

To serve, unmold onto a serving platter, cut into wedges, and spoon some of the caramel sauce over each serving.

Persimmon Pudding

Plums there are of three sorts. The red and white are like our hedge plums. but the other which they call *putchamins*, grow as high as a palmetto: the fruit is like a medlar; it is first green, then yellow, and red when it is ripe; if it be not ripe, it will draw a man's mouth awry, with much torment, but when it is ripe, it is as delicious as an apricot.

John Smith

No doubt but putchamins are what we call the persimmon, for what else can so pucker the mouth short of alum? Folk wisdom cautions against eating the fruit before frost, though it can ripen as early as late August in northern Florida. Settlers also called it an American date from the natives' drying of it. The Indians also pounded it with dried meat, nuts, and other berries to make a nutritious traveler's food, pemmican, which is still used on arctic and antarctic expeditions. Our species of the persimmon is *Diospyros virginiana; Diospyros kaki* is its oriental cousin frequently found in grocery stores, but it lacks the intense flavor and dense texture necessary for successful cooking.

Yields 4 to 6 servings

1 quart (1 L) very ripe
  persimmons
2 cups (475 ml) buttermilk
4 ounces (115 g) butter
1½ cups (302 g) sugar
3 eggs
1½ cups (183 g) flour
½ teaspoon salt

1 teaspoon baking soda
1 teaspoon baking powder
½ teaspoon freshly grated
  nutmeg
½ teaspoon ground ginger
1 teaspoon ground cinnamon
Butter for the pan
Boiling water for the bain-marie

Recommended equipment: A colander or food mill; electric mixer; rubber spatula; baking dish or loaf pan, and a larger pan for forming a bain-marie.

Butter the baking dish or loaf pan and preheat oven to 325°F (163°C).

Pass the persimmons through a food mill or colander to obtain 2 cups or so of pulp. Stir the buttermilk into the fruit. In a separate bowl, beat the butter well and gradually add the sugar. Beat in the eggs separately and then beat in the fruit until well mixed. Sift the dry ingredients twice—flour, salt, baking soda, baking powder, nutmeg, ginger, and cinnamon. Fold the dry ingredients into the liquid ingredients until well mixed. Pour the batter into the smaller, greased dish or pan. Set this pan into the larger one and add enough boiling water around it to measure 1 inch (2½ cm). Bake on middle level of the preheated oven for about 1 hour. The eggs should be set, but the pudding should remain very moist. Serve it warm or cold with whipped cream or Custard Sauce (see page 157).

❧ Wine Jelly ❧

Charles Knox made a standard gelatin powder commercially available in the 1890s and since then has come an unbroken string of rather common and often vulgar congealed desserts. At one time, though, gelatin dishes—wine jellies, charlotte russes—were considered very elegant. A recipe from 1756 found in the notebook of the legendary Charleston female planter Eliza Lucas Pinckney gives an idea of the travail behind the elegance, and the honor bestowed upon a guest whose hostess had gone to so much trouble: "When I make the Jelly with sweetmeats I put two Calves foot, half a pound of hartshorn shavings, and an ounce of Isinglass, into five pints of spring water, let it boil over a slow fire till it comes to three. . . ." (Hartshorn was, since the Middle Ages, a source of gelatin from antlers; isinglass a source derived from the air bladders of fish.)

The recipe below for wine jelly is remarkably delicate—the gelatin holding all in fragile suspension until the flavors are immediately dispersed at the heat of the palate. If it is necessary to unmold, you will need to double the amount of gelatin—and you will have also quite a different, though good, dessert. This dish of English tradition is, in a typically English fashion, often served with vanilla pound cake and a custard sauce.

2 tablespoons unflavored, unsweetened gelatin
1/4 cup (60 ml) cold water
1 1/4 cups (295 ml) cold water
Zest of 1 lemon, in strips
Zest of 2 oranges, in strips
1 1/2 inch (3 3/4 cm) piece of cinnamon stick

1 cup (202 g) sugar
Juice of 2 large oranges and 2 lemons (total to equal 1 1/8 cups or 295 ml)
1 1/2 cups (355 ml) Amontillado sherry

Recommended equipment: A 1 1/2-quart (1 1/2 L) heavy-bottomed saucepan, swivel-bladed peeler for removing the zest, strainer.

Dissolve the gelatin in the 1/4 cup cold water in the bottom of a stainless steel or glass mixing bowl. Set aside.

Prepare the syrup by combining 1 1/4 cups of cold water with the orange and lemon zests, cinnamon stick, and sugar. Bring to a boil in the saucepan over medium heat. Strain and add to gelatin, stirring well. Cool to room temperature, then add the fruit juices and the sherry. Chill in the dishes you wish to serve from, either wine glasses or a large serving bowl, as this dessert is too delicate to unmold. Serve with Custard Sauce (recipe follows) or whipped cream and a plain cookie or pound cake.

❧ Custard Sauce ❧

Yields approximately 1 1/4 cups

1/2 cup (118 ml) half-and-half
1/2 cup (118 ml) milk
3 egg yolks

2 to 3 tablespoons sugar
Salt
1 teaspoon vanilla extract

Recommended equipment: A double boiler.

Combine the half-and-half, milk, egg yolks, sugar, and a pinch of salt in the top of a double boiler set over, not in, hot water on medium heat. Cook, stirring constantly, until the sauce is thickened by the cooking of the egg yolks. Remove from heat and stir in the vanilla extract. Serve warm or cold.

Elliott and Madeline, my two youngest children, call this old-fashioned cobbler "pig pie," as I always cut the biscuit dough with a pig-shaped cookie cutter. In North Carolina, if we're lucky, this is our dessert on the Fourth of July, for the first blackberries and peaches are just showing up in the farmers' market. It's a recipe only for the summer; though you can vary the given proportions, only fresh fruit—not canned or frozen—will make a successful pie.

Yields 8 servings

The fruit

2 tablespoons butter
3 cups (710 ml) peeled, sliced
   peaches
4 cups (950 ml) blueberries

1 cup (235 ml) blackberries
4 tablespoons flour
2 cups (403 g) sugar
1/4 teaspoon cinnamon

Butter biscuits

2 cups (244 g) flour
1 teaspoon salt
1 tablespoon sugar
3 1/2 teaspoons baking powder
6 tablespoons butter

1/2 cup (118 ml) milk
1/4 cup (60 ml) heavy cream
Flour for rolling out biscuits
Sugar for sprinkling biscuits

Recommended equipment: A baking dish, medium mixing bowl, pastry blender, rolling pin, 2 1/4-inch (5 3/4 cm) biscuit cutter or any cookie cutter.

Preheat oven to 425°F (218°C).

Grease the baking dish well with the 2 tablespoons of butter. Combine the fruits, flour, sugar, and cinnamon in the mixing bowl and toss well but very gently. Pour into the baking dish.

Make the biscuits by sifting the flour, salt, sugar, and baking powder together. Cut the butter into the dough using the fingertips or a pastry blender. Stir the milk and cream into the dough with 10 to 12 quick strokes and turn onto a floured surface. Knead lightly and roll out to a 1/2 inch (1 1/4 cm) thickness. Cut dough with cutter and sprinkle the tops with granulated sugar. Place the biscuits on top of the fruit

Desserts

and bake for about 35 minutes or until biscuits are lightly browned. Serve with whipped cream, vanilla ice cream, or alone.

⟿ Pie Pastry ⟿

For 8 ounces (225 g) of dough

Yields one 9-inch (22½ cm) pie crust

1 cup (122 g) flour	2 tablespoons (30 g) lard
½ teaspoon salt	2 to 3 tablespoons *cold* water
1 teaspoon sugar	Flour for rolling out dough
2 tablespoons (30 g) butter	

For 12 ounces (340 g) of dough

Yields one 10-inch (25 cm) pie crust or a larger, thin tart shell

1½ cups (183 g) flour	3 tablespoons (45 g) lard
¾ teaspoon salt	3 to 5 tablespoons *cold* water
1½ teaspoons sugar	Flour for rolling out dough
3 tablespoons (45 g) butter	

Recommended equipment: A sifter, pastry blender, waxed paper.

Sift the flour, salt, and sugar together into a mixing bowl. Cut the butter and lard into ½-inch (1¼ cm) squares. Add to the flour and refrigerate for 15 minutes. Remove from the refrigerator and incorporate the fat into the flour with the fingertips or a blending fork. Work quickly and lightly. All the flour should be cream colored (no longer white) and coarse as cornmeal, but the fat may remain in small pellets. Sprinkle the cold water over and bind, using a fork. Pat the dough together into a cake, wrap airtight in waxed paper or plastic, and refrigerate for 30 minutes before rolling out.

For a partially baked pastry shell

Recommended equipment: Aluminum foil, 1 pound (450 g) dried beans or rice.

After chilling, roll out dough thinly on a lightly floured surface, form into pan (or pans), and return to refrigerator to chill for 30 minutes.

Preheat oven to 375°F (190°C). Remove pans from refrigerator and line the pie shell with aluminum foil, pressing gently against the edges so the crust will maintain its edge. Distribute 1 pound (450 g) of dried beans or rice in the aluminum foil. Bake for 10 minutes on lowest level of oven, carefully remove the foil and beans, and bake 5 more minutes, or until the dough no longer seems raw, but has a light crust. It is now ready for the filling. (The beans or rice may be reused for future crusts by letting them cool and keeping them in a dry container with lid, such as a coffee can.)

 Chess Pie

In Tennessee, as many as six or seven of these pies, once baked and cooled, are stacked on each other and sliced as a cake. Elsewhere they are offered singly, with a little whipped cream.

Yields 6 to 8 servings

1 recipe Pie Pastry for 8 ounces (225 g) of dough, partially baked (see page 159)	7 tablespoons (105 g) butter at room temperature
1¼ cups (252 g) sugar	3 large eggs
Salt	1 large lemon, zest finely grated and juice strained

Recommended equipment: An electric mixer, 9-inch (22½ cm) pie pan.

Preheat oven to 325°F (163°C).

Beat the sugar, a pinch of salt, and butter together until light. Add the eggs one by one, beating well after each addition, then add the zest and juice of the lemon. Pour the mixture into the partially baked shell and cook about 35 minutes on the middle level of the oven until the custard is set. The top should brown lightly but not puff.

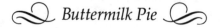 Buttermilk Pie

Buttermilk pie is a lighter, tangier version of the more commonly encountered chess pie.

Yields 6 to 8 servings

½ cup (115 g) butter	3 eggs, separated
1⅓ cups (269 g) sugar	3 tablespoons flour

1½ cups (355 ml) buttermilk
1 tablespoon lemon juice
½ teaspoon freshly grated
  nutmeg

Salt
1 recipe Pie Pastry for 8 ounces
  (225 g) of dough, partially
  baked (see page 159)

Recommended equipment: An electric mixer, rubber spatula, 9-inch (22½ cm) pie pan.

Preheat oven to 325°F (163°C).

   Cream the butter and sugar well and add the egg yolks, one by one. Beat in flour and buttermilk and add the lemon juice and nutmeg with a pinch of salt. Whip the egg whites until stiff and fold into the filling. Pour the filling into the partially baked pie pastry and cook in the middle level of the preheated oven until the custard is set and slightly brown, about 1 hour. Serve topped with fresh fruit such as peaches, strawberries, or blueberries and slightly sweetened whipped cream. Fresh fruit sauces are also excellent with this (see recipes).

❧ *Green Tomato Tart* ❧

Southerners can't seem to make up their minds whether tomatoes are fruits or vegetables, and they bring them to the table in all sorts of guises, from soups, to side dishes, to pickles, to pies. If there is a use for those hard, barely blushed supermarket tomatoes, it would be as a substitute for the green tomatoes in this recipe.

Yields 8 to 10 servings

1 recipe Pie Pastry for 12 ounces
  (340 g) of dough, partially
  baked (see page 159)
1 pound (450 g) firm, green
  tomatoes
2 cups (403 g) sugar

2 tablespoons flour
½ teaspoon ground ginger
¼ teaspoon ground cinnamon
Juice and grated zest of 1 lemon
2 eggs, well beaten
1½ tablespoons (23 g) butter

Recommended equipment: An 11-inch (28 cm) tart pan or two 8-inch (20 cm) cake pans, 3-quart (3 L) saucepan, colander, stainless steel box grater.

Pastry shell
Prepare the pie pastry according to the master recipe, giving it 30 minutes to chill. Then roll out thinly for either one large tart or two

smaller ones. Form dough into the pans and chill in pans for 30 minutes.

Preheat oven to 375°F (190°C).

Green tomato filling

Blanch the tomatoes in boiling water in the saucepan for 1½ minutes, immerse in cold water, and peel. If the skin is hard to remove, a swivel blade vegetable peeler will remove it nicely. Slice the tomatoes thinly, then chop roughly, and put in a colander to drain for 10 minutes.

Sift the sugar with the flour, ginger, and cinnamon to ensure an even mixture. Turn into a bowl and toss with the drained tomatoes. Add the lemon zest and juice, and the beaten eggs and stir well. Pour into the pastry shell and bake on middle level of the oven for 30 minutes, or until eggs are set. Serve warm with lightly whipped, lightly sweetened cream.

ᏩᎧ *Double Crust Apple Pie* ᏩᎧ

The warm, dry air of Indian summer is especially appreciated by those who have lived through the humid haze of August on a southern farm. By the end of September, vegetables and fruits will dry in the sun, and my grandmother carried out clean, white sheets covered with fragrant apple slices each morning and rolled them up to come inside each evening. In the winter, when she made her double crust apple pie, we could relive those perfect autumn days.

Yields 6 servings

Crust

2 recipes Pie Pastry for 8 ounces
    (225 g) of dough, for total of 16
    ounces (450 g), chilled (see
    page 159)
Flour for rolling

Filling

4 ounces (115 g) dried apples	⅔ cup (134 g) sugar
3 cups (710 ml) water	Salt
½ teaspoon powdered cinnamon	4 eggs

2 tablespoons (30 g) butter
Butter for greasing the pan
1 tablespoon sugar

Recommended equipment: A 9-inch (22½ cm) pie pan, 1½-quart (1½ L) saucepan with lid, colander, mixing bowl, pastry brush.

Combine the apples and water in the saucepan and bring to a boil. Turn off the heat and let sit, covered, for 30 minutes. Drain in the colander and turn into a mixing bowl. Sprinkle with the cinnamon, sugar, and salt and beat well. Separate one of the eggs and reserve the white for the glaze. Add that yolk and the three whole eggs to the apple mixture along with the butter and beat well again.

Preheat oven to 350°F (177°C).

Prepare the pan by greasing it lightly with butter. Roll out one-half of the dough (8 ounces or 225 g) on a lightly floured surface to an 11-inch (27½ cm) diameter. Fit it into the pan and add the filling. Roll out the other half of the dough and drape it over the top of the pie. Dampen the edges and crimp the two crusts together, sealing well. Beat the reserved egg white with 1 tablespoon water. Brush the top of the dough well with the egg white and sprinkle the 1 tablespoon sugar over the surface. Cut 8 to 12 small slits in the top crust so steam can escape as the pie bakes. Bake in the middle level of the preheated oven for about 1 hour or until the crust is golden brown. Serve hot with whipped cream. This pie reheats well.

❧ Sweet Potato Pie ❧

Henry VIII, always in the market for an improvement in his love life, set the fashion for sweet potatoes at the English court in the sixteenth century. He voraciously consumed staggering amounts baked in spiced pies, believing tales of their aphrodisiacal powers. The sweet potato, its attributes unproved, lasted in favor about as long as one of Henry's wives. Today in Europe its consumption is limited mainly to Spain, where it was introduced from the New World as early as 1493. In the American South it still finds much favor as a vegetable or baked, as for the king, in a pie.

Yields 6 to 8 servings

Crust

1 recipe Pie Pastry for 8 ounces
(225 g) of dough, partially
baked (see page 159)

Filling

1 cup to 1¼ cups (235 to 295 ml)
cooked, riced sweet potatoes (1
large or 2 small tubers)
4 ounces (115 g) butter
¾ cup (151 g) light brown sugar
3 eggs, separated
¾ cup (180 ml) milk

¼ teaspoon salt
¼ teaspoon freshly grated
nutmeg
¼ teaspoon ground cloves
½ teaspoon ground cinnamon
¼ cup (60 ml) Bourbon or dark
rum

Topping

4 tablespoons butter
4 tablespoons brown sugar
4 tablespoons flour
4 tablespoons chopped pecans

Note: The sweet potatoes may be baked in their skins in the oven or peeled and boiled until tender.

Recommended equipment: An electric mixer, potato ricer, 9-inch (22½ cm) pie pan, rubber spatula.

Preheat oven to 375°F (190°C).

Cream the butter with the light brown sugar and add the mashed sweet potatoes. Beat in the egg yolks and milk. Add salt, nutmeg, cloves, and cinnamon for seasoning, and beat in the Bourbon or rum. In a separate clean bowl, with clean beaters, whip the egg whites until stiff. Add one quarter of the whites to the potato custard and stir in well. Gently fold the remaining whites into the mixture and pour into the partially baked pie shell. Prepare the topping by beating the butter, brown sugar, flour, and nuts together until just mixed. Sprinkle over the pie, and bake on the middle level of the preheated oven until the top is golden brown and the eggs are set, about 40 minutes.

Macy's Chocolate Meringue Pie

This was my favorite dessert as a child, and it used to be quite common at church suppers, school fairs, and cake sales. I rarely see it anymore; the South's taste in chocolate has followed the rest of the nation's to excess in over-rich truffles, designer brownies, and so forth.

1 recipe Pie Pastry for 8 ounces (225 g) of dough, prebaked (see page 159)	1 tablespoon flour
	Pinch salt
	2½ cups (590 ml) milk
3 ounces (84 g) unsweetened chocolate	3 egg yolks
	1½ teaspoons vanilla
¾ cup (151 g) sugar	3 egg whites
3 tablespoons cornstarch	6 tablespoons sugar

Recommended equipment: A double boiler, medium saucepan, electric mixer.

Prepare the pie pastry and cook it until it is completely done, about 20 minutes in all. Cool on a rack.

Melt the chocolate in the double boiler over simmering water.

Mix the sugar, cornstarch, flour, and salt thoroughly. Stir in the milk and cook, while stirring, until the mixture thickens. Add the melted chocolate to the sauce. Beat the egg yolks with a little of the hot mixture, then beat them into the rest of the chocolate mixture. Cook 2 or 3 minutes, stirring constantly. Remove from heat and beat in the vanilla.

Preheat oven to 325°F (163°C).

Beat the egg whites until frothy, then slowly add the sugar. Beat until stiff peaks form. Pour the chocolate custard into the pie shell. Spread the meringue over the top and bake for 10 to 15 minutes or until the meringue is golden brown. Cool, then refrigerate.

Huguenot Torte

If I had to choose only one cake as my favorite, it would unquestionably be this Huguenot torte from Charleston. The layers are so light from the well-beaten eggs, yet so rich and moist from the pecans and apples that it seems a contradiction, a palpable cloud. The Creole combination of a classic French technique and the native pecan is inspired. There is great reward in eating this cake, beyond its flavor and texture, though, a symbolic participation in the French Huguenots' success in finally securing religious freedom. The rights and privileges granted them under Henri IV were systematically usurped by Cardinal Richelieu upon the king's death. Louis XIV extended the persecution. In the 1680s, their number in France fell by a million; families fled across Europe, to England, and to North America. Nowhere were the expatriate Huguenots more successful than in the Low Country of South Carolina, nowhere did they maintain their cultural and religious identity longer. Much of the fine food of that region is the legacy of the Huguenot search for freedom.

Yields 6 to 8 servings

The torte

1½ cups (355 ml) shelled pecans (6 ounces or 170 g, by weight)
2 medium-sized cooking apples
3 eggs (at room temperature)
1 cup (202 g) sugar

½ cup (61 g) flour
2 teaspoons baking powder
½ teaspoon salt
1 teaspoon vanilla extract

Assembly

8 perfect pecan halves
Cold water
Granulated sugar

⅔ cup (160 ml) whipping cream, chilled
1 teaspoon sugar
½ teaspoon vanilla extract

Recommended equipment: Two 9-inch (22½ cm) cake pans; parchment, waxed or brown paper for lining pans; nut grinder, food processor, or blender; hand or stationary mixer; rubber spatula.

Prepare the cake pans by lightly greasing them, lining the bottoms with paper, greasing the paper, and lightly dusting the pans with flour.

Preheat oven to 325°F (163°C).

Grind the pecans to a fine mill in the grinder, blender, or food processor. Proceed in small batches; blending too long will heat the nuts and render them oily. Peel the apples, quarter, core, and chop very fine. Cover and reserve. Proceed quickly with the recipe so that it will not be necessary to add lemon juice to the fruit.

In a bowl or the bowl of the mixer, beat the eggs until doubled in volume. Slowly add the sugar while beating, and continue until volume is tripled. Eggs should be very thick and light in color. Sift the flour with the baking powder and salt over the egg mixture. Sprinkle the ground pecans over all, followed by the apples and vanilla. With a large spatula, fold the mixture together rapidly, being certain to incorporate the elements all the way to the bottom of the bowl. Divide batter between the two cake pans and bake in the middle level of the preheated oven for about 35 minutes. When done, the sides will pull away slightly. Place on a rack and let cool for 20 minutes.

Meanwhile, lightly toast the pecan halves under a broiler. While hot, quickly dip in water and then roll them in a little granulated sugar sprinkled on a plate until they are lightly coated. Let them dry on a rack.

Assembly

The cake layers must be perfectly cool or the heat will melt the cream. Invert the pans to remove the cake, discard the paper liners, and invert again so the crusty, top baked surface is in its original position. Choose one layer for the top of the cake, placing the other on a serving platter.

Whip the chilled cream with 1 teaspoon granulated sugar and ½ teaspoon vanilla extract until stiff. Cover the bottom layer with a little more than half of this cream. Carefully position the top layer. Pipe rosettes or add dollops of whipped cream around the edges. Garnish with the glazed pecans and serve chilled.

↶ Chocolate Black Walnut Pound Cake ↷

The native black walnut trees were doubly important for early settlers. The hard, fine-grained wood was used in much of the better, and now prized, frontier furniture. The extremely oily nuts were often employed in cooking. The taste is pervasive, paling its cousin, the English walnut.

Yields 10 to 12 servings

4 ounces (115 g) semisweet chocolate, melted	4 eggs
	1½ teaspoons vanilla extract
1 cup (225 g) butter	1¾ cups (160 g) sifted cake flour
1 cup (202 g) sugar plus 2 tablespoons	¼ teaspoon salt
	1¼ teaspoons baking powder

¼ teaspoon baking soda
1 cup (235 ml) buttermilk
½ cup (118 ml) black walnuts,
    lightly toasted
Butter and flour for pan

Recommended equipment: A double boiler, loaf pan, brown paper, electric mixer.

Preheat oven to 325°F (163°C).

Measure all ingredients and bring to room temperature. Melt the chocolate in the top of a double boiler over hot water. Line the bottom of the loaf pan with brown paper. Grease the paper and the sides of the pan with butter and dust the whole interior lightly with flour.

Beat the butter well and gradually add the sugar until the mixture is creamed and very light and fluffy. Add the eggs one at a time, beating well after each addition. Beat in the vanilla. Sift the flour, salt, baking powder, and soda together. Add the sifted flour mixture to the butter mixture in three parts, alternating with the buttermilk. Stir the batter well after each addition until smooth. Add the melted chocolate and toasted nuts and fold just enough to mix evenly. Pour into the lined loaf pan.

Place in the middle level of the preheated oven and bake for about 1 hour and 10 minutes, or until a clean straw or toothpick inserted into the center of the cake comes out clean (the center should be moist but not liquid). Remove the cake from the oven, place it in its pan on a rack, and let rest 10 minutes; then turn out to finish cooling. Serve warm or cold with very slightly sweetened whipped cream or Custard Sauce (see page 157). This cake keeps very well and is delicious toasted with butter.

∾ *Toasted Pecan Caramel Cake* ∾

At any southern church supper, social, or dinner on the grounds, a caramel cake will most likely vanish before any other dessert. The perfect caramel cake—without the slightest grain to the icing—is respected by all cooks; it is particularly relished by the southern male. Its appearance is no everyday occurrence either, being reserved for Sundays, birthdays, or holidays. The slightly astringent quality of the pecan is much to my taste. In this cake it works well to play against the intense sweetness of the praline icing.

Yields 12 servings

The layers

1 cup (225 g) butter
2 cups (403 g) sugar
4 eggs, separated
2 cups (244 g) flour
3/4 cup (180 ml) finely ground
  pecans

2 1/4 teaspoons baking powder
1/2 teaspoon salt
1 cup (235 ml) milk
1 1/2 teaspoons vanilla extract
Butter and flour for the pans

Recommended equipment: A nut grinder, food processor, or blender; electric mixer; two mixing bowls; rubber spatula; three 9-inch (22 1/2 cm) cake pans.

Preheat oven to 350°F (177°C).

Grind the pecans to a fine mill in the grinder, food processor, or blender. Proceed in small batches; blending too long will heat the nuts and render them oily.

Butter and flour the three baking pans. All ingredients should be at room temperature. Cream the butter well and gradually beat in the sugar. Add the egg yolks one by one, reserving the whites for the final step. Sift the flour, ground pecans, baking powder, and salt together. Add one-third of the mix to the butter, sugar, and eggs. Add 1/2 cup (118 ml) of the milk, one-third of the dry ingredients, the remaining milk, then the remaining dry ingredients. Mix well and add vanilla extract. In a separate, clean bowl beat the egg whites until stiff. Fold one-fourth of the egg whites into the batter, stirring well. Gently fold the remaining whites into the batter and pour the batter into the cake pans. Bake 30 to 35 minutes. The cakes will be lightly browned and drawn away from the edges of the pans. Let cool 5 minutes and turn out onto a cooling rack.

The icing and garnish

1 pound (450 g) light brown
  sugar
1 cup (235 ml) heavy cream
1/8 teaspoon salt
1 tablespoon light corn syrup

6 tablespoons (90 g) butter
1 teaspoon vanilla extract
48 perfect pecan halves
1 tablespoon (15 g) butter
1 teaspoon granulated sugar

Recommended equipment: A 1 1/2-quart (1 1/2 L) heavy-bottomed saucepan with lid, candy thermometer, electric mixer, icing spatula.

Preheat oven to 400°F (204°C).

Combine the brown sugar, heavy cream, salt, and corn syrup in the saucepan and bring to a boil over medium high heat, stirring constantly. At the boil, cover the pot and cook 3 minutes. Uncover and cook rapidly until the candy thermometer reaches 242°F (117°C)—this is the upper limit of the soft ball stage, almost at hard ball if you do not have a thermometer. At this point remove from heat and beat in 2 tablespoons cold butter. Let icing cool to lukewarm.

While waiting for the icing to cool, roast the pecans with the 1 tablespoon of butter for 10 minutes in the oven. Remove, sprinkle with sugar, and return to the oven for 2 more minutes. Let cool and reserve.

When icing is lukewarm, beat in vanilla extract and the remaining 4 tablespoons of butter. Continue beating until icing thickens somewhat. It should remain fairly glossy and smooth. (If icing cools too much, its texture and gloss can be restored by reheating very gently with a little cream or milk.) When ready, ice cake and decorate top with reserved pecans.

∾ Lady Baltimore Cake ☙

Though Owen Wister spread the fame of Lady Baltimore across the country with his well-known book of the same name, it is probably truer today that the enduring charm of the confection has led more people to seek out the 1906 novel than vice versa. While the Women's Exchange no longer exists—the site of an intrigue wherein aristocratic family secrets are revealed in the book—this old-fashioned cake is still available on special request from the Olde Colony Bakery at 280 King Street in Charleston. Mr. and Mrs. Peter Kikos, still baking after more than thirty years' experience, offer several traditional Low Country baked goods, including an excellent benne seed wafer, pecan pies and tarts, the Huguenot torte, the Charleston whipped cream cake, and the opulent plantation-style fruit cake, coated in marzipan and iced in buttercream. Mrs. Kikos says the Lady Baltimore is "too soft to ship," but she will package it for travel.

Yields 12 servings

The layers

½ cup (115 g) butter
1 cup (202 g) sugar

2 cups (244 g) flour
2 teaspoons baking powder

^{1}/$_{2}$ cup (118 ml) milk
^{1}/$_{2}$ teaspoon almond extract
4 eggs, separated
Butter for greasing the pans

Recommended equipment: Three 9-inch (22^{1}/$_{2}$ cm) cake pans, electric mixer, rubber spatula, 1^{1}/$_{2}$-quart (1^{1}/$_{2}$ L) heavy-bottomed saucepan, candy thermometer, icing spatula.

Preheat oven to 375°F (190°C) and butter the three cake pans.

Beat the butter well, until light. Gradually add sugar and continue beating until well creamed. Sift the flour and baking powder together. Add the dry ingredients and the milk alternately, beginning and ending with the flour. Add the almond extract and the 4 egg yolks. Beat the whites, separately, in a clean bowl with clean beaters until stiff. Gently fold one-fourth of the beaten whites into the batter and incorporate well. Add the remaining egg whites and fold in gently. Pour into the cake pans and bake in middle level of the preheated oven for 20 to 25 minutes, until the top is golden and the edges pull away from the pan. Let cool in the pan for a short while and turn out onto a rack to cool completely.

The syrup

^{1}/$_{2}$ cup (101 g) sugar
^{1}/$_{2}$ cup (118 ml) water
Zest of one lemon
Juice of one lemon
1 teaspoon vanilla extract

Boil the sugar, water, and lemon zest together in the saucepan for five minutes. Let cool; add the lemon juice and vanilla extract. Spoon over the cooled layers.

The icing

1 cup (235 ml) raisins
1 cup (235 ml) English walnuts, broken
^{1}/$_{2}$ cup (118 ml) sherry, rum, brandy, or Bourbon

2 cups (403 g) sugar
^{1}/$_{4}$ cup (60 ml) water
4 egg whites
1 teaspoon vanilla extract

Let the raisins and nuts macerate in the sherry or other alcohol for 20 minutes in a glass or ceramic bowl. Combine the sugar and water in the clean saucepan for a syrup to be cooked to 246°F (119°C), the hard ball stage. While the syrup cooks, beat the egg whites separately with the mixer until almost stiff, with soft peaks just beginning to form. At that moment, pour the boiling syrup over the egg whites in a thin stream, beating constantly. Continue beating until the icing thickens, then add the vanilla extract, the raisins, nuts, and any unabsorbed liquid. Ice the cake with the meringue, between the layers, and over the outside.

ᥱ Tipsy Parson ᥲ

Tipsy Parson comes directly from the eighteenth-century repertoire. In eastern Virginia, Maryland, and the Carolinas, the recipes for it are heirlooms, and the execution of the dish is the prerogative of the family matron. The closely related trifle is probably the best known of these drunken confections. As the name indicates, Tipsy Parson makes extravagant use of wine, custard, and cream on Sundays, holidays, and family festivities.

6 eggs, separated
1½ cups (300 g) sugar
1¾ cups (210 g) flour
¼ teaspoon salt
½ cup (115 ml) milk
1½ to 2 cups (352 ml) sherry
1 recipe Custard Sauce (see page 157)

1½ cup (352 ml) whole blanched almonds, raw or lightly toasted if desired
1 pint whipping cream
3 tablespoons sugar
¼ cup (60 ml) sherry

Recommended equipment: Three 9-inch (22½ cm) cake pans, buttered and floured; electric mixer.

Preheat oven to 325°F (163°C).

Beat the egg yolks well and gradually add the sugar until the mixture is tripled in volume. Sift the flour and salt together and sprinkle over the egg yolks. Fold lightly, then add the milk. Beat the egg whites until stiff. Fold into the batter and divide among the 3 pans. Bake at 325°F (163°C) for about 20 minutes. Remove and cool on a rack a few minutes before turning out.

To assemble the cake, place one layer on a cake stand or platter. Soak well with sherry and cover with one half the custard. Repeat with the second layer. Top with the third and soak it well too. Stud the cake all over with the whole almonds. Whip the cream to soft peaks, add the sugar and sherry, and beat until fairly stiff peaks form. Do not overbeat. Heap the cream luxuriously all over the cake. Refrigerate for 2 hours before serving.

ᴄ᷂ Three Confections from New Orleans ᴄ᷂

Beignets, pralines, and calas are three sweetmeats that belong solely to New Orleans in the popular imagination. Generations of Creoles and now tourists have ended nights of revelry at the Café du Monde in the French Quarter with a heavy white china mug full of café au lait and a plate of sugar-dusted fritters freshly fried. These beignets are as popular as ever, though the other two sweets have suffered less kind fates. Once the little candies called pralines were sold on the street by the pralinières who made them in their own kitchens in great variety—white and pink coconut, almond, and pecan. Now, the praline is the victim of the modern food industry: coconut oil is often used instead of pure, fresh butter, corn syrups instead of cane sugar. At one time, the black women who mastered the tricky calas sold them hot for breakfast. These calas ladies are gone also; the rice cake that they brought from Africa has almost disappeared as well.

ᴄ᷂ Beignets ᴄ᷂

Yields 6 to 8 servings

1 cup (235 ml) water
1/2 cup (115 g) butter
1/4 teaspoon salt
1 1/2 tablespoons sugar
1 cup (122 g) flour
4 eggs (at room temperature)

1 1/2 teaspoons vanilla extract
3 to 4 tablespoons brandy,
    Calvados, or dark rum
Vegetable shortening or peanut
    oil for deep frying
Powdered sugar

Optional: cinnamon

Recommended equipment: A 1 1/2-quart (1 1/2 L) saucepan, deep fryer or 12-inch (30 cm) cast-iron skillet, frying thermometer, slotted spoon, brown paper bag.

Combine the water and butter in the saucepan and bring to a full boil. Sift the salt, sugar, and flour together. Add to the boiling liquid all at once and stir well over medium heat for 4 to 5 minutes, or until the dough is smooth, glossy, and comes away from the sides of the pan. Remove from heat and stir for 2 to 3 minutes to cool slightly. Incorporate the eggs into the mixture, one at a time, beating vigorously after each addition until well blended. Beat in the vanilla and the brandy or rum.

To fry
Heat the shortening or oil in the deep fryer or skillet to 360°F (182°C). Use two teaspoons to form the fritters. First, quickly dip them in the hot oil, then take up a small amount of dough with one spoon, and release it into the fat using the back of the other spoon as a scraper. Dip both spoons into the fat, form another fritter, and repeat until the surface of the oil is occupied. The fritters will rise to the top and cook on one side until they flip over and cook on the other side. (While frying, be sure to maintain as even a temperature as possible; oil which cools too quickly from the addition of cold ingredients will make greasy beignets, and oil which is too hot will burn the fritters.) When golden brown all over, remove with a slotted spoon to drain on brown paper bag and dust with powdered sugar or powdered sugar mixed with a little cinnamon. Serve as soon as possible.

⎯⎯ Bourbon Pecan Pralines ⎯⎯

Yields approximately 24 candies

2 ounces (60 g) butter
1 cup (202 g) sugar
1 cup (202 g) light brown sugar, packed
Salt
½ cup (118 ml) heavy cream

2 cups (475 ml) pecan halves, lightly toasted
2 teaspoons vanilla extract
1 to 2 tablespoons Bourbon
Butter for greasing cookie sheet

Recommended equipment: A 1½-quart (1½ L) heavy-bottomed saucepan with lid, candy thermometer, baking sheet.

Butter the baking sheet lightly.

Melt the butter over low heat in the heavy-bottomed saucepan. Stir in the sugars, a pinch of salt, and cream. Cover and bring to a boil over medium heat. Remove the lid and boil rapidly until temperature reaches 242°F (117°C) on the thermometer. (This is the upper limit of the soft ball stage in cooking sugar; a drop of syrup in chilled water will hold its shape well.) At this point, add the toasted pecans and stir well. Remove from heat and beat in flavorings. Continue beating until candy loses its glossiness, becomes creamy in appearance, and starts to thicken. Quickly drop the mixture by tablespoons onto the greased cookie sheet. If pralines aren't to be used soon after preparation, store them by wrapping individually in foil or plastic wrap.

∾ Calas ∾

Yields approximately 24 cakes

1 cup (235 ml) cold, cooked rice
1 cup (235 ml) stale white bread crumbs from either French-style bread or biscuits
2 teaspoons baking powder
½ teaspoon cinnamon
⅛ teaspoon freshly grated nutmeg
2 tablespoons sugar

1 to 2 tablespoons chopped glacéed or dried fruit (optional)
1 egg
2 tablespoons heavy cream
1 teaspoon vanilla extract
Powdered sugar
Peanut oil or vegetable shortening for deep frying

Recommended equipment: A deep fryer or 12-inch (30 cm) cast-iron skillet, frying thermometer, slotted spoon, brown paper bag.

Combine the rice with the bread crumbs, baking powder, cinnamon, nutmeg, and sugar. (Stir in optional chopped fruit if desired.) Beat the egg with the cream and vanilla and fold into the other ingredients. Let rest for 15 minutes.

Heat the oil or shortening in the deep fryer or skillet to 360°F (182°C) on the thermometer.

Roll the mixture into small balls, approximately 1¼ inches (3 cm) in diameter, and fry in the oil. The calas will rise to the surface and turn as they cook to a golden brown. (While frying, be sure to maintain as even a temperature as possible; oil which cools too quickly from the addition of cold ingredients will not fry properly, and oil which is too hot will burn the calas.) Remove them from the oil with a slotted spoon and drain on brown paper bag. Serve hot, sprinkled with powdered sugar.

German influence in southern culture is often underestimated, but it began with Queen Anne's active support of German emigration, providing transportation from England to Pennsylvania for many who were seeking economic and religious freedom. In Pennsylvania they were known as the Pennsylvania Dutch, from *Deutsch* meaning German. As the better farmlands were taken there, they moved south down the Great Wagon Road from Philadelphia, settling in the piedmont sections of Maryland, Virginia, and North and South Carolina. They spoke German and maintained their cultural heritage. A German printer in Salisbury, North Carolina, distributed tracts in the native language on a wide scale. *Random Recollections of a Long Life* by Edwin J. Scott records many of the German traditions that survived in the South Carolina frontier; their cooking was praised: "as for soups and fried cakes, the Germans had more and better varieties than any other nationalities in our country." The German influence is now most obvious in the architecture of Old Salem, North Carolina, originally settled in 1752. Many eighteenth- and nineteenth-century buildings have been restored there; one—Winkler's Bakery—still prepares many traditional Moravian baked goods in an enormous wood-fired oven.

Yields at least 16 dozen cookies

3 tablespoons (45 g) lard	3 cups (366 g) flour
4 tablespoons (60 g) butter	½ tablespoon ground cloves
¾ cup (151 g) light brown sugar	1 tablespoon ground ginger
¼ cup (60 ml) honey	2 tablespoons ground cinnamon
⅔ cup (160 ml) sorghum molasses (or cane molasses as a substitute)	⅔ teaspoon salt
	1 teaspoon baking soda
2 tablespoons brandy	Flour for rolling the cookies
2 tablespoons boiling water	Butter for the pan

Recommended equipment: An electric mixer, sifter, rolling pin, baking sheet, cookie cutters.

Combine the lard and butter and beat well. Add the brown sugar to cream well, and beat in the honey and molasses. Add the brandy and water to the mixture. Sift the flour with the cloves, ginger, cinnamon, salt, and baking soda. Resift the flour into the mixture in the bowl and work in with a wooden spoon. At some point it will be necessary to roll up your sleeves and work the dough by hand until well mixed. Cover and chill the dough at least 3 hours, but preferably overnight.

Preheat oven to 375°F (190°C).

Using as little flour as possible, roll out small portions of the dough to a thickness less than ⅛ inch (⅓ cm). You cannot roll these wafers too thin. Cut into desired shapes; circles, stars, crescents, and animals are traditional. Bake on a greased cookie sheet for 4 to 7 minutes until brown at the edge. *Do not overcook, as the spices will become bitter.* Cool on a rack until crisp. These Christmas cookies store well in an airtight container. Just before baking, the wafers may be lightly sprinkled with granulated sugar.

 *Peach Sauce*

This fresh fruit sauce and the one that follows can top off ice cream, pound cake, rice pudding, chess and buttermilk pies, pancakes, waffles, and bread pudding.

Yields about 2 cups

5 large, ripe peaches weighing
   approximately 1½ pounds
   (675 g)
Juice of 1 lemon
½ to ¾ cup (101 to 151 g) sugar

Recommended equipment: Two saucepans, one 1½ quart (1½ L) and one 3 quarts (3 L); fine-mesh strainer; pestle or wooden spoon.

Blanch the peaches in boiling water in the large saucepan for 45 seconds. Refresh in cold water, peel, and slice into the small saucepan. Sprinkle with the lemon juice and add sugar. (The amount of sugar required will vary with the sweetness of the peaches.) Bring to a boil in the saucepan over high heat, stirring. Reduce heat and simmer for 15 minutes. Rub through the strainer with the back of a wooden spoon or with a pestle. Refrigerate if not used immediately.

❧ Two Berry Sauce ❧

Yields about 3 cups

¼ cup (60 ml) water
½ cup (101 g) sugar
Juice of 1 lemon

1 cup (235 ml) fresh raspberries
and 2 cups (475 ml) fresh
strawberries
(or 3 cups fresh strawberries if
raspberries are unavailable)

Recommended equipment: A 1½-quart (1½ L) saucepan.

Boil the water, sugar, and lemon juice together for 5 minutes. Mash the berries roughly and add to the syrup. Boil rapidly for 3 more minutes, then cool to room temperature. Refrigerate if not used immediately.

❧ Raspberry Fool ❧

In the South we have so many traditions to choose from in the kitchen that it is easy to take the best of each. The French and African influences are most important in our savory dishes, and the English in our home baking and desserts. We have nogs and possets, trifles, slips, and fools—all essentially unchanged from the original recipes of the British Isles. A fool, as we know, is simple. As a dessert, it is only fresh fruit, raw or lightly stewed, strained, and folded into rich cream. Frozen fools were the preferred ice creams of the South through the mid-nineteenth century. The French or custard-based ice creams were used only when the cream was not rich enough to carry the dish. In the last few years health food stores ironically have begun to carry richer, more authentic "heavy creams." It is worth the effort to seek out these products in all cooking, and especially for fools, with only three or four ingredients in relief. Strawberries, blueberries, blackberries, peaches, and figs may be used alone or in combination.

Yields 4 to 6 servings

½ cup (101 g) sugar
1½ to 2 cups (350–470 ml) fresh
    raspberries
1 cup (235 ml) heavy cream

Recommended equipment: A small saucepan with lid, fine mesh, sieve or strainer, electric mixer.

Heat the sugar in the saucepan until it is hot to the touch. Reserve a few whole raspberries for garnish, and add the rest to the sugar. Cover, shake well and remove from heat. Stir occasionally to dissolve the sugar, cool to room temperature. Rub through a sieve or strainer to remove the seeds. Refrigerate the purée until cold.

Beat the cream to stiff peaks. Stir about ¼ of it into the fruit. Fold in the rest of the cream in two parts. Chill well before serving. Use individual ramekins or dessert glasses, or serve at the table from a large glass bowl set over ice.

 Vanilla Brandy

Vanilla Brandy is more delicious and aromatic than the extract in the stores. It is made from the whole seed pods of *Vanilla fragrans,* a member of the orchid family and a native of the American tropics. True vanilla has an expensive, fine and pervasive flavor; synthetic vanilla is only pervasive and cheap. The longevity of the true pod, though, reduces its initial cost substantially. Covered in brandy or sugar, the pods can provide flavor for several years as the jars are topped off again after use.

4 vanilla beans
12 ounces (355 ml) good brandy

Split the beans lengthwise, then cut into thirds. Put in a jar and pour the brandy over. Cover and shake well. Store in a cool dark place for four weeks, shaking vigorously as you remember it. Replace whatever is used with an equal amount of brandy. Lasts several years.

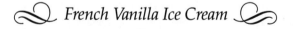 French Vanilla Ice Cream

When I was very young, making ice cream was a very involved process. The cow had to be milked and the eggs gathered before the custard could be made. If we wanted strawberries we had to pick them. For ice, we piled into the back of the pickup and headed four miles away to the Blacksburg Ice Company. On the loading dock, big men split steaming two-foot-thick slabs of ice into blocks and tossed them into deafening grinders. The frozen pellets shot into our galvanized tubs, and we carried away our already disappearing treasure.

Back home, all of us children wanted to churn at first. Usually cousins had come over for the treat, and we pushed and shoved to get a turn. Once the churning got serious, the prize was the seat on top of the churn; it took the weight of a child to hold the freezer steady while adult strength kept the dasher moving.

I think such memories are precious, not because of a sweet tooth, but because they are memories of an entire family, both sexes, all ages, working happily together toward one end—from the children picking fruit to the women making custard to the men wrestling with the churn. It's a sweet thought even without the ice cream.

Today, I have an Italian-made machine with a self-contained electric compressor. There are no trips to the ice plant, but I still use my mother's recipe for custard ice cream.

Yields 1 quart

2½ cups (590 ml) milk	Pinch salt
1 cup (235 ml) cream	2 to 3 tablespoons Vanilla Brandy
8 egg yolks	(see page 179)
1 cup (210 g) plus 1 tablespoon	1 cup (235 ml) cream
sugar	

Recommended equipment: A medium saucepan, double boiler, ice cream freezer.

Heat the milk and 1 cup cream in the saucepan. In the top of the double boiler, beat the egg yolks vigorously with the sugar and salt. Slowly add the warm milk to the yolks, and set over simmering water. Stir constantly until the custard thickens slightly, is hot to the touch, and all taste of raw egg is dissipated. Remove from the heat, cool completely, and add the vanilla brandy. Stir in the remaining 1 cup cream and freeze according to the manufacturer's directions.

⤴ Fig Ice Cream ⤵

Since I moved to Chapel Hill, fig ice cream has become less and less a reality. Fig trees will survive the winters here but are often frozen back to the ground. The drought of three summers running has done more damage. My two-year-old fig tree set fruit this year, but by August the figs were dried on the vine.

Nancy Tolley shares her figs with me for the picking. Her two trees were planted by the Tottens about sixty years ago. Dr. Totten was a renowned horticulturist and botanist, and the figs were among the first plants he and his wife Annie set out on the property, putting them in even before construction on the house began. Nancy has well water to maintain the garden, but the drought was so severe this year that she had to resort to "strategic watering." The strategy didn't include watering the fig tree.

When we first moved to Chapel Hill, farmers would bring paper trays full of luscious little brown figs to Fowler's Food Store in late August and September. That was when a good number of Chapel Hill ladies in white gloves shopped with their maids. Clearly, I was too new to town and too obviously a college student to participate in this ritual. However, I took the figs within reach and went blind as a mule to the checkout line.

Yields 1 quart

3 cups (700 ml) fresh figs
Sugar
Juice of 1 lemon
1 recipe French Vanilla Ice Cream
  (see page 179)

Peel the figs and mash them roughly. Sweeten to taste with sugar and stir in the lemon juice. Let stand 15 minutes, then add to the custard for French Vanilla Ice Cream. Freeze accordingly. Serve with a little Port poured over the dessert.

Southern Spirits

When we were old enough to learn that in Mississippi, despite its being a dry state, you could order liquor and have it delivered anywhere at any hour of the day, we had a case of Jack Daniels sent to the Tuesday meeting of the Baptist ladies, and watched from the shrubbery while Harry, of the Top-of-the-Hill "Grocery," was berated, stampeded, and torn apart by the ladies when they caught sight of his cargo. "You . . . you . . . Get out of here!" the president cried, and Harry, more frightened of physical injury than fearing a waste of good sour mash, swooped up the case and escaped in fast order.

Willie Morris, *North Toward Home*

Bourbon

Whiskey in etymological meaning takes its place alongside aquavit, both meaning the water of life. Technically, it is a highly alcoholic beverage distilled from fermented grain. In the American South the abundant grain was corn, and thus came corn whiskey. Thomas Amy wrote of corn in 1682 that the Carolina settlers "have lately invented a way of making with it good sound Beer; but it's strong and heady. By maceration, when duly fermented, a strong spirit like Brandy may be drawn off from it, by the help of an Alembick." The name Bourbon came about later. Elijah Craig's mill in Georgetown, Bourbon County, Kentucky, furnished ground corn for a liquor called Bourbon County whiskey, and the name soon was applied to all whiskey distilled partially or wholly from corn. Today, the mash must be 51 percent corn to carry the name Bourbon. The term sour mash refers to yeast used in fermentation; no less than one-fourth of the yeast used must come from a previous fermentation. It is analogous to the sour-dough bread process, and its adherents are equally loyal. (Tennessee whiskey is not necessarily made from a majority of corn mash; wheat or rye may predominate, but it is always distilled in Tennessee.) Two famous southern drinks are based on corn whiskey: one, the julep, draws on the English heritage; the other, Sazerac, on the French.

Juleps have a long history coming from the English "cup" tradition of serving mixed alcoholic beverages flavored with cooling seasonings such as mint, lovage, cucumber, or fruit in the summer. These were especially welcomed during the long, hot months of the American South and were naturalized by the adoption of corn whiskey. Mint, which grows so easily and reliably, gained preeminence as the flavoring. A man more pugilistic than I might insist on one classic formula for the mint julep. I would rather offer *un Marseillais* a few hints on Bouillabaisse. The recipe here makes a good julep, the one I favor, and I'll let it go at that! Later, the mint julep was reintroduced to England by a South Carolinian, and Oxford celebrates that good fortune with a Mint Julep Day each June.

The Sazerac reflects the French influence in New Orleans, combining the Mediterranean taste for anise and the southern penchant for corn. A flavored sugar cube is found at the bottom of this cup, as it is in many New Orleans drinks, the most famous being café brulot. Bitters were eagerly adopted by the Creoles, the French always ready for yet another *digestif.* This thoroughly hybrid drink, the Sazerac, was the specialty of the famed St. Charles Hotel and, according to legend, took its name from a celebrated bartender.

❧ Mint Julep ☙
Yields 1 julep

2 teaspoons sugar
2 teaspoons water
6 to 8 mint leaves
Finely crushed ice
2 ounces (60 ml) Bourbon

Recommended equipment: A silver goblet or a tumbler (approximately 7 ounces or 215 ml).

Combine the sugar, water, and mint leaves in the bottom of a silver goblet or tumbler. Crush the mint gently with the back of a spoon; it is not necessary for the sugar to dissolve. Add approximately ³/₈ cup (95 ml) dry, finely crushed ice and pour the Bourbon over. Do not stir or shake, but let stand a few minutes until the container frosts over.

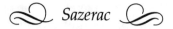 Sazerac

Herbsaint is the locally produced, New Orleans version of Pernod.

Yields 1 Sazerac

1 teaspoon Herbsaint or Pernod	Strip of lemon zest
1 lump of sugar	Crushed ice
3 to 4 drops of Peychaud bitters	2 ounces (60 ml) Bourbon

Recommended equipment: An old-fashioned glass (a tumbler, approximately 7 ounces or 215 ml).

Put the Herbsaint or Pernod in the glass and rotate until interior is completely coated with the liqueur. You may pour out the excess if desired. Put the lump of sugar in the bottom of the glass and splash the bitters over it. Crush the sugar with the back of a spoon, add a strip of lemon zest, and fill glass two-thirds full with dry, crushed ice. Pour the Bourbon over, give the glass a twirl, but not a stir, and serve.

Scuppernong Wine

The southern colonies bore the heavy burden of unrealistic English expectations. In this sunny, warm land, silk was to be produced and spices grown to diminish the economic importance of the Orient. Grapes and olives were to break dependence on the Continent. John Smith, typically, raised great hopes for wine production: "Except by the rivers and savage habitations, where they are not overshadowed from the sun, they are covered with fruit, though never pruned nor manured. of those hedge grapes we made near twenty gallons of wine, which was like our French British wine, but certainly they would prove good were they well manured."

The scuppernong, though, never found acceptance as a table wine, being too assertive to marry well with foods. As an aperitif this wine is more acceptable. It also can be used well in cooking—a chicken, duck, or pork roast basted with it will be a rich golden brown and yield a pan full of delicious drippings for a sauce.

Yields about 3 quarts

4 quarts (4 L) ripe scuppernong grapes
1 quart (1 L) boiling water
1 pound (450 g) sugar

²/₃ cup (160 ml) good brandy (not a sweetened or fruit brandy) or vodka

Recommended equipment: A stoneware crock with lid, potato masher or ricer, cheesecloth, loose-mesh strainer, bottles or jars for storing wine.

Wash the grapes well, let them drain, and place them in a stoneware crock. Crush well with a potato masher or ricer. Pour the boiling water over the fruit: skins, pulp, and juice. Secure a double thickness of cheesecloth over the top of the crock and let rest in a cool, dark place for 24 hours. Day 2: Add 1 pound sugar, stir well, re-cover, and store for 24 hours as above. Day 3: Strain out the pulp, seeds, and skins, pressing well to extract all juices. Re-cover and store as above. Days 4, 5, 6: Let rest. Day 7: Skim off and discard all foam from the top of the fermenting juice. Strain through a triple thickness of clean cheesecloth until clear. Add ²/₃ cup brandy or vodka and cover tightly with a lid. Let rest 2 days. On day 9, draw off (by siphoning if possible), and bottle in dry sterile containers. Store in a cool, dark place for 3 months before using.

This simplified recipe will probably be helpful:
Day 1: Crush grapes, add water, store covered with cheesecloth.
Day 2: Add sugar, store covered with cheesecloth.
Day 3: Strain and store covered with cheesecloth.
Days 4–6: Store covered with cheesecloth.
Day 7: Skim, strain, add brandy, store covered tightly.
Day 8: Store covered tightly.
Day 9: Draw off and bottle.

Ratafias and Cordials

Ratafias are infused, sweet beverages of high alcoholic content that enjoyed great popularity in the eighteenth and nineteenth centuries. Most were homemade due to the ease of manufacture: ratafias (and all cordials) are merely compounded from already distilled liquors; that is, there is no complicated distillation process. Rather, flavorings are added to the alcohol and left to infuse for a time. Later, the liquid is strained and sweetened, usually by a syrup since sugar's ability to dissolve is crippled in the presence of alcohol. The French and English used brandy to carry their flavors, as did many southerners. A particularly American adaptation is the orange cordial based on corn whiskey. Oranges were more common in earlier days than one would expect. Before Florida was acquired and the citrus groves developed there, oranges and lemons were cultivated from Louisiana to South Carolina. In 1831, *New England Magazine* published a report of the Charleston Market: "There are oranges, the growth of Carolina, and the earth produces few larger or better." These oranges were often part of a spectrum of fruits and flavorings used alone or in combination for cordials: nutmeg, juniper berries, cinnamon, aniseed, angelica, coriander, orange blossoms, jessamine blossoms, strawberries, raspberries, plums, sour cherries, pomegranates, currants, green walnuts, and vanilla.

At first, ratafias were considered of medicinal value, taken to improve the circulation. Later, before the invention of the polite cocktail, they became a stock parlor drink for ladies in an age when the coarseness of strong alcoholic drink was denied to a supposedly weaker sex. The name eventually became archaic, but the drinks are increasingly popular today, providing a less expensive alternative to many imported liqueurs.

ℒ *Blackberry Cordial* ℒ

Yields approximately 8 quarts

7 quarts (6¼ L) fresh, ripe
   blackberries
5 cups (1185 ml) water

5 pounds (2¼ kg) sugar
Zest of 5 lemons, in strips
1 gallon (3½ L) brandy or vodka

Recommended equipment: A swivel-bladed peeler or sharp paring knife, a 4-gallon (15 L) stoneware crock, a 4-quart (4 L) stainless steel saucepan.

Pick over the blackberries, but avoid washing them unless absolutely necessary. Put them into a stoneware crock. Peel the zest from the lemons, being careful to get as little of the white pith as possible. Over medium high heat boil the water with the sugar and lemon zest in the saucepan until the sugar is completely dissolved, approximately 10 minutes after it comes to the boil.

Pour immediately over the berries and let stand 12 hours. Add the brandy or vodka and cover. Store in a cool, dark place for 4 weeks. Strain through clean, wet cheesecloth, but do not force the berries. Bottle in sterilized bottles or jars, but do not vacuum seal. Store in a cool, dark place for at least 2 more months before using.

◁ *Peach Kernel Ratafia (Noyaux)* ◁▷

A recipe calling for 8 ounces of peach kernels may seem impractical at first, but what better excuse to indulge yourself at the height of the fresh peach season? Two dozen peaches can supply this amount; and you can add the kernels as you collect them—they need not be added all at once, and a few extra won't hurt. Modern large freestone peaches are an excellent choice: the stone splits easily to yield the nutlike kernel. This ratafia of French origin was one of the most popular throughout the southern states. Its name, noyaux or noyan, reflects the almondlike flavor imparted.

Yields 3 pints

8 ounces (225 g) peach kernels—
    the nut inside the stone
1 quart (1 L) brandy
1 pound (450 g) sugar
2 cups (475 ml) water

Optional: 24 fresh, clean, dry peach leaves.

Recommended equipment: A glass or stoneware crock; three 1-pint (500 ml) glass bottles or jars.

Bruise the peach kernels by rapping them with the flat side of a kitchen knife and add to the brandy in a glass or stoneware crock. Store covered in a cool, dark place for 3 weeks. Add the peach leaves, if available, stir well, and store for another week. At the end of this 4-week period, make a syrup by boiling the water and sugar. Add to the brandy, stir well, and store overnight. The next day, strain and bottle, storing in a cool, dark place for 6 more weeks before serving.

Orange Cordial

Yields about 1 quart

8 oranges
2 lemons
1 fifth (750 ml) good Bourbon
   whiskey

²/₃ to 1¹/₃ cups (160 to 315 ml)
   sugar
¹/₂ cup (118 ml) water

Recommended equipment: A swivel-bladed peeler, stoneware crock, 1¹/₂-quart (1¹/₂ L) heavy-bottomed saucepan, two 1-pint (500 ml) glass bottles or jars.

Take the zest from the oranges and lemons with the peeler, leaving no white attached. Put it in a stoneware (or glass) crock and cover with the Bourbon. Cover the container and let sit in a cool, dark place for six weeks. Strain and discard the fruit peel. Boil the sugar and water together until sugar is dissolved. Cool to room temperature. Add to the whiskey, stir well, and bottle. Return to the storage place; serve after 4 more weeks.

Eggnog

Anna Wells Rutledge wrote the introduction to the facsimile of the 1847 edition of *The Carolina Housewife,* the most important of the early southern cookbooks. She quotes a Philadelphian writing home in 1842: "Before breakfast, at Christmas time, everyone takes a glass of egg-nog and a slice of cake. It is the universal custom and was not on this occasion omitted by anyone. As Christmas was kept during four days egg-nog was drank regularly every morning." The nog is one of the most widespread of southern holiday traditions, but it is not only a festive beverage: its ritual consumption on Christmas morning guarantees peace and good cheer for the coming New Year.

Yields 16 cups

6 egg yolks
¹/₃ cup (67 g) sugar
1 cup (235 ml) rum
1 cup (235 ml) Bourbon

1 cup (235 ml) brandy
2 cups (470 ml) milk
2 cups (470 ml) cream
Nutmeg for grating

Recommended equipment: A large glass or stainless steel bowl, whisk, nutmeg grater.

The day before serving, beat the eggs with the sugar until very light and tripled in volume. Slowly whisk in the liquors. Store in a cool place or refrigerate overnight. Before serving, stir in the milk. Beat the cream to light peaks and fold in. Grate a little nutmeg over each cup when it is served.

⟨Q⟩ St. Cecilia Punch ⟨Q⟩

A small subscription concert given in 1737 in Charleston, South Carolina, in honor of St. Cecilia's Day marked the founding of America's first musical society. Today a prestigious ball preserving antebellum-style hospitality is the only remnant of the culturally ambitious society. Mrs. St. Julien Ravenel wrote: "each and all have it on their consciences to see that all goes well,—that no guest is overlooked, no lady neglected, no stranger unwelcomed." Immediately after the Civil War, refreshments were spartan. Rose Ravenel made her debut during those years. "There were two long tables at the side of the room covered with fine damask, large dishes of biscuits, silver coffee pots. Biscuits and coffee were handed around." At the successive parties of that season, "we would meet at each other's houses and dance. We had nothing to eat, only water to drink. This went on for years."

Now prosperity has returned champagne to the ball. A green tea punch has been long associated with the St. Cecilia, its elements reflecting the makeup of the old Charleston aristocracy—the tea for the English, champagne for the French, and the tropical fruits and rum for the West Indies planters.

Yields 60 to 75 servings

6 to 8 lemons
1 750-ml bottle of brandy
1 quart (1 L) water
4 cups (1 L) sugar
8 tablespoons green tea leaves
1 pineapple

1 750-ml bottle dark rum
5 750-ml bottles dry (brut) champagne
2 to 4 750-ml bottles seltzer water
Ice in large block

Recommended equipment: 2 large glass or ceramic mixing bowls, 3-quart (3 L) heavy-bottomed saucepan, large punch bowl.

Slice the lemons as thinly as possible, put into a large glass or ceramic bowl, and macerate overnight in the brandy. The next day bring the water and sugar to a rapid boil over medium heat in the saucepan. Pour over the tea in the second mixing bowl and let stand until cool. Peel, core, and slice thinly the pineapple. Add it to the lemon and brandy, strain the tea into it, and pour into the punch bowl. Pour in the dark rum and let stand (chilling if possible) until ready to serve when the champagne and seltzer are added.

Add the block of ice to the punch bowl and serve. Do not serve with crushed ice as it will dilute and greatly diminish the flavor.

Kitchen Equipment

All the equipment recommended in the recipes follows. No special tools, pots, or pans are needed for any of the dishes, but it is helpful to know what size pot to get out before you start cooking. All items should be heavy, durable ware; a good source is a professional hotel and restaurant supply store. If you're buying in any quantity, more than two or three large items, do not hesitate to ask for a discount. You may not get one, but many stores will cooperate. Other than cast iron for skillets, most cooking surfaces should be inert: glazed porcelain, glass, stainless steel, tin, or enamel. Heavy aluminum is fine for baking and roasting pans; it will not do for any sort of pickling process. If you cannot afford an excellent, heavy-bottomed stainless steel stockpot, buy a thin enamel one and some sort of "flame tamer" and never turn your back on it, for fear of scorching. I recommend putting your money into good pots and pans rather than any number of electrical appliances. I use a blender for puréeing and grinding nuts and coffee, an eighteen-year-old hand mixer for whipping cream, and arm power for everything else. This list is also an almost complete census of my kitchen, and I have cooked dinners for as many as twenty people with the equipment at hand.

Saucepans

1½ quart (1½ L) with lid
3 quart (3 L) with lid
4 to 5 quart (4 to 5 L) with lid
Double boiler insert for one of the above saucepans

Stockpots

8 quart and 16 quart (8 and 15 L) with lids

Skillets

8-, 10-, and 12-inch (20, 25, and 30 cm) cast-iron or enameled cast-iron. For seasoning new cast-iron cookware, see page 121.

Baking and roasting pans

Cake pans (3)—9 inches (22½ cm)
Pie pan—9 inches (22½ cm)

Tart pan—11 inches (27½ cm)

Cooling racks (2)

Baking dishes (2)—11 × 7 × 2 inches (27½ × 17½ × 5 cm)

Baking sheet—11 × 15 inches (27½ × 37½ cm)

Glass or ceramic soufflé dish— 2 quarts (2 L)

Tube pan—9 or 10 inches (22½ or 25 cm)

Loaf pan—9¼ × 5¼ × 2¾ inches (23½ × 13⅓ × 7 cm)

Dutch oven—7 to 8 quarts (7 to 8 L)

Heavy roasting pan—about 11 × 15 inches (27½ × 37½ cm)

Knives

2-inch (5 cm) paring knife

5-inch (12½ cm) flexible-bladed boning knife

8-inch (20 cm) chef's knife

Heavy cleaver—about 1 pound (450 g)

Small ware

Fine-mesh wire strainers (2)—3½ and 6 inches (8¾ and 15 cm) in diameter

Metal colander—about 9 inches (22½ cm) in diameter

Piano wire whisk—about 10 to 12 inches (25 to 30 cm) in length

Wooden whisk

Potato masher or ricer

Swivel-bladed vegetable peeler

Garlic press

Wooden spoons (2)

Metal slotted spoon

Oven thermometer

Instant-read meat thermometer

Candy thermometer

Frying thermometer

Poultry shears

Stainless steel box grater

Pepper grinder

Pastry brush with natural bristles

Flexible icing spatula—6 inches (15 cm)

Large rubber spatula—about 12 inches (30 cm) in length

Flat turning spatula

Metal tongs

Flour sifter

Biscuit cutters (2)—1 inch and 2¼ inches (2½ and 5¾ cm) in diameter

Cookie cutters

Pastry blender or blending fork

Stiff natural bristle brush

Ladle with 10-inch (25 cm) long handle

Hardwood rolling pin

Marble mortar and pestle

Large pastry bag and tips

Stainless steel funnel

Mixing bowls

2 quart (2 L)

4 quart (4 L)

8 quart (8 L)

Supplies

Brown paper bags
Waxed paper
Cheesecloth
Hardwood charcoal
Hickory chips

Special equipment

For canning:
Open kettle canner with rack and
    lid
Rubber tipped tongs
3- to 4-gallon (12 to 15 L)
    stoneware crock with lid

Other:
5-gallon (20 L) stoneware crock
Charcoal grill with a minimum of
    144 square inches (365 cm²) of
    cooking area
Electric deep fryer with
    thermostat

Appliances

Blender
Food mill
Meat grinder and sausage horn
Hand mixer
Stationary mixer with processing
    attachments or food processor

Works Consulted

Arber, Edward, ed. *Travels and Works of Captain John Smith*. 2 vols. Edinburgh: John Grant, 1910.

Beverly, Robert. *Virginia; The History and Present State of Virginia*. Edited by Louis B. Wright. Chapel Hill, N.C.: University of North Carolina Press, 1947.

Bowes, Frederick P. *The Culture of Early Charleston*. Chapel Hill, N.C.: University of North Carolina Press, 1942.

Brown, William Wells. *My Southern Home*. 1880. Reprint. New York: Negro Universities Press, 1969.

Chopin, Kate. *A Night in Acadie*. Chicago: Way and Williams, 1897.

Eustis, Célestine. *Cooking in Old Créole Days*. Facsimile reprint. New York: Arno Press, 1973.

Fields, Mamie Garvin. *Lemon Swamp and Other Places*. New York: Free Press, 1983.

Foner, Philip S. *History of Black Americans*. Westport, Conn.: Greenwood Press, 1975.

Foxfire 10, no. 4 (Winter 1976).

G. M. "South Carolina." *New England Magazine* 1 (Sept. 1831).

Gordon, Caroline. *The Collected Stories of Caroline Gordon*. New York: Farrar Straus Giroux, 1981.

Grimé, William, ed. *Ethno-Botany of the Black Americans*. Algonac, Mich.: Reference Publications, 1979.

Hammond Harwood House. *Maryland's Way*. Annapolis: Hammond Harwood House Assn., 1963.

Hilliard, Sam Bowers. *Hog Meat and Hoecake*. Carbondale, Ill.: Southern Illinois University Press, 1972.

Hudson, Charles. *The Southeastern Indians*. Knoxville, Tenn.: University of Tennessee Press, 1976.

Junior League of Charleston. *Charleston Receipts*. Charleston, S.C.: Walker, Evans, and Cogswell, 1950.

Junior League of Savannah. *Savannah Style*. N.p.: Kingsport Press, 1980.

Kephart, Horace. *Camp Cookery.* New York: Macmillan Co., 1931.

——. *Our Southern Highlanders.* New York: Macmillan Co., 1914.

Larson, Lewis H. *Aboriginal Subsistence Technology.* Gainesville, Fla.: University of Florida Press, 1980.

Leslie, Eliza. *Miss Leslie's New Cookery Book.* Philadelphia: T. R. Peterson, 1857.

McCullers, Carson. *The Ballad of the Sad Café, The Novels and Stories of Carson McCullers.* Cambridge, Mass.: Riverside Press, n.d.

Manteo Women's Club. *Roanoke Island Cook Book.* N.p. 1978.

Marszalek, John F., ed. *The Dairy of Miss Emma Holmes 1861–1866.* Baton Rouge, La.: Louisiana State University Press, 1979.

Montagné, Prosper. *The New Larousse Gastronomique.* New York: Crown Publishers, 1977.

Morris, Willie. *North Toward Home.* Oxford, Miss: Yoknapatawpha Press, 1967.

Parker, Cherry, and Bradsher, Frances. *The Hand-Me-Down Cookbook.* Durham, N.C.: Moore Publishing Co., 1969.

Parris, John. *Mountain Cooking.* Asheville, N.C.: Asheville Citizen-Times Publishing Co., 1978.

Porcher, F. P. *Resources of the Southern Fields & Forests, Medical, Economical and Agricultural.* Charleston, S.C.: Evans & Cogswell, 1863.

Randolph, Mary. *The Virginia Housewife.* Washington, D.C.: Thompson, 1828.

Ravenel, Mrs. St. Julien. *Charleston.* New York: Macmillan Co., 1906.

Recipe Book of Eliza Lucas Pinckney 1756. Charleston, S.C.: Charleston Lithographing Co., 1936.

Rhett, Blanche S. *Two Hundred Years of Charleston Cooking.* Edited by Lettie Gay. Columbia, S.C.: University of South Carolina Press, 1976.

Robbins, Maria Polushkin, ed. *The Cook's Quotation Book.* Wainscott, N.Y.: Pushcart Press, 1983.

Rose P. Ravenel's Cookbook. N.p. Lellyett and Rogers, 1983.

Rutledge, Sarah. *The Carolina Housewife.* Facsimile edition. Columbia, S.C.: University of South Carolina Press, 1979.

Scott, Edwin J. *Random Recollections of a Long Life.* Columbia, S.C.: Charles A. Calvo, Jr., Printer, 1884.

Simms, William Gilmore. "Summer Travel in the South." *Southern Quarterly Review* n.s. 2 (Sept. 1850). New Orleans, The Proprietors, 1842–1857.

Smith, D. E. Huger. *A Charlestonian's Recollections, 1846–1913.* Charleston, S.C.: Carolina Art Association, Walker, Evans & Cogswell, 1950.

Solomon, Jack and Olivia. *Cracklin' Bread and Asfidity.* University, Ala.: University of Alabama Press, 1979.

Southern Agriculturist and Register of Rural Affairs. Charleston, S.C.

Taylor, Joe Gray. *Eating, Drinking and Visiting in the South.* Baton Rouge, La.: Louisiana State University Press, 1982.

The Picayune's Creole Cook Book. New York: Dover Publications, 1971.

"Topographical and Historical Description of the County of Brunswick, in North Carolina." *National Register* 1 (27 July 1816).

Trillin, Calvin. *Third Helpings.* New Haven, Conn.: Ticknor and Fields, 1983.

Ulmer, Mary, and Beck, Samuel E., eds. *Cherokee Cooklore.* N.p.: Museum of the Cherokee Indian, 1951.

Walthall, John A. *Prehistoric Indians of the Southeast.* University, Ala.: University of Alabama Press, 1980.

Waring, Laura Witte. *The Way It Was in Charleston.* Old Greenwich, Conn: Devin-Adair Company.

Washington, Booker T. *Up from Slavery.* New York: A. L. Burt Co., 1900.

Welty, Eudora. *The Bride of the Innisfallen.* New York: Harcourt, Brace and Co., 1955.

———. *A Curtain of Green.* New York: Harcourt, Brace and Co., 1941.

Wister, Owen. *Lady Baltimore.* New York: Macmillan Co., 1906.

Wolfe, Thomas. *Look Homeward, Angel.* New York: Charles Scribner's Sons, 1952.

Woodmason, Charles. *The Carolina Back Country on the Eve of the Revolution.* Edited by Richard J. Hooker. Chapel Hill, N.C.: University of North Carolina Press, 1953.

◁ Index ▷

Bold numbers indicate recipe entries

A

Africans, black, 63, 150, 173; diet of, 3, 5, 8, 9, 66, 71
Andouille, 49, 51–52
Apples: fried, **68**; dried, in pie, 162; in torte, 165
Artichokes, Jerusalem, 130
Aspic, 8, 109, **140**
Awendaw, **32**

B

Baked tomatoes, **60**
Baltimore, Md., 14, 114
Barbecue, 102, 103; sauce, **103**
Bath, England, 36
Beans, 25; red, 49; butter, 60; favas, 60; in egg sauce, **60**; October, 60; pole, 60; snap, 60; lima, 60, 78; dried, **67**; fried cakes, **68**
Bear, black, 125–26
Beaufort, N.C., 44
Beef: in southern cooking, 104–5; country style steak, **106**; grillades and grits, **106**; en daube glacé, **108**; Natchitoches meat pies, **110**
Beignets, **173**; okra, **71**. *See also* Fritters
Beverages: mint julep, 183, **184**; Sazerac, 183, **184**; scuppernong wine, **184**; ratafias 185–87; cor-

dials, 186, 188; eggnog, **188**; St. Cecilia punch, **189**
Biscuits, 33–34; beaten, **34**; raised, **35**; angel or bride's, **36**, 82; butter, **158**
Blackberries, 158, 186
Black-eyed peas, 66–68; hoppin' John, **43**
Blueberries, 158
Boeuf en daube glacé, **108**
Boiled dressing, **134**, 136
Bourbon, 182–84, 188
Bourbon pecan pralines, **174**
Braised greens, **62**
Bread: spoon, 3, 25, **29**; dog, 25, **26**; Sally Lunn, **36**; Moravian sugar, **38**; rice (Philpy), **44**; chestnut spoon, **131**. *See also* Biscuits; Corn bread
Breaux Bridge, La., 12
Brunswick stew, 6, **20**
Burgoo, 6, **22**
Butter biscuits, **188**
Buttermilk, 27, 28, 36, 45, 118, 122, 132, 155, 167; corn bread, **28**; pie, **160**

C

Cabbage pudding, **57**; in coleslaw, 136
Cafe du Monde, 173
Cajuns, 11, 106